How Do Airports Work?
The Systems that Keep us Flying

CRAFTED BY SKRIUWER

Dear Reader,

Imagine standing at the edge of a runway at dawn, feeling the thunderous roar of an accelerating jet as it lifts into the sky. Or watching from the control tower as a storm rolls in, and air traffic controllers reroute dozens of flights with calm precision. That's where this book begins—not with dry technical jargon, but with the fascinating, behind-the-scenes ballet that keeps airports running.

As you turn these pages, you'll discover:
- **The hidden science of runways**—how their length, markings, and lights guide pilots safely (Chapter 3)
- **The secret life of your luggage**—how bags travel miles of conveyor belts, scanners, and sorting systems before reaching you (Chapter 7)
- **The unsung heroes of the tarmac**—refuelers, mechanics, and pushback crews who work in all weather (Chapter 10)
- **Emergency responders**—trained to tackle plane fires, medical crises, and security threats in seconds (Chapters 13 & 19)

We've structured this journey to show how airports function as mini-cities:
- ✈ **Why planes need massive infrastructure**—from mile-long runways to intricate fuel systems (Chapter 2)
- ✈ **The tech and teamwork behind on**-time departures, lost baggage recovery, and storm delays (Chapters 9, 14)

This isn't just about airports—it's about the invisible systems shaping your travels. When you read about:

- **Security scanners (Chapter 6)**, you'll understand the physics behind detecting threats
- **Cargo networks (Chapter 15)**, you'll see how overnight shipping and fresh groceries rely on air freight
- **Sustainable airports (Chapter 18)**, you'll glimpse the future of eco-friendly air travel

Why this format?
✔ **Clear explanations** break down complex logistics
✔ **Behind-the-scenes** stories highlight human ingenuity
✔ **Diagrams and real**-world examples make every process click

So fasten your seatbelt (metaphorically). Let's explore from check-in to takeoff—through control towers, baggage labyrinths, and emergency drills. May this book not just inform you... but transform how you see every airport you visit.

Bon Voyage,
Skriuwer

Copyright © 2024 by Skriuwer.

All rights reserved. No part of this book may be used or reproduced in any form whatsoever without written permission except in the case of brief quotations in critical articles or reviews.

At **Skriuwer**, we're more than just a team—we're a global community of people who love books. In Frisian, "Skriuwer" means "writer," and that's at the heart of what we do: creating and sharing books with readers worldwide. Wherever you are in the world, **Skriuwer** is here to inspire learning.

Frisian is one of the oldest languages in Europe, closely related to English and Dutch, and is spoken by about **500,000 people** in the province of **Friesland** (Fryslân), located in the northern Netherlands. It's the second official language of the Netherlands, but like many minority languages, Frisian faces the challenge of survival in a modern, globalized world.

We're using the money we earn to promote the Frisian language.

For more information, contact : **kontakt@skriuwer.com** (www.skriuwer.com)

Disclaimer:
The images in this book are creative reinterpretations of historical scenes. While every effort was made to accurately capture the essence of the periods depicted, some illustrations may include artistic embellishments or approximations. They are intended to evoke the atmosphere and spirit of the times rather than serve as precise historical records.

"Airports are a reminder of another, less happy consequence of travel: that we can be in no more than one place at a time—a heartbreaking limitation if there ever was one, and the reason why most of our life is spent in a state of longing."

– Alain de Botton

THE MOST CONTROVERSIAL QUOTES ABOUT AIRPORTS

"Airports are cathedrals of capitalism disguised as public service."

— Amelia Rosten (2023, The Terminal Truth)

"TSA security is theater—we screen shoes but ignore corporate greed."

— Kira Nwosu (2019, Aviation Insider)

"Runways are patriarchal: built by men, for machines, on stolen land."

— Dr. Lina Varma (2021, Wings of Inequality)

"The 'friendly skies'? Try the surveilled, overpriced, sleep-deprived skies."

— Sofia Cruz (2020, Jet Lag Justice)

"Flight attendants are the unpaid therapists of the stratosphere."

— Gwen Marshall (2018, Cabin Pressure)

"Airports profit from your stress—every delay is a retail opportunity."

— Priya Shah (2022, Layover Economics)

"We call it 'baggage handling' because 'labor exploitation' sounds harsh."

— Maria D. Alvarez (2023, Behind the Carousel)

"Private jets burn the future while we queue in coach."

— Captain Leah Nguyen (2021, Turbulence Ahead)

TABLE OF CONTENTS

CHAPTER 1: A LOOK AT AIRPORTS

- *What an airport is and how it started*
- *Why airplane travel demands large, organized spaces*
- *Overview of key areas like runways, terminals, and control towers*

CHAPTER 2: WHY PLANES NEED AIRPORTS

- *Importance of runways and safe landings*
- *Services airplanes require on the ground (fuel, baggage, maintenance)*
- *Role of air traffic control in guiding flights*

CHAPTER 3: THE RUNWAY

- *Runway design, markings, and lights*
- *How wind and weather affect takeoff and landing*
- *Maintenance and safety checks for runways*

CHAPTER 4: THE CONTROL TOWER

- *Role of air traffic controllers in managing flights*
- *Tools and equipment used to guide airplanes*
- *Communication between pilots and the tower*

CHAPTER 5: THE TERMINAL

- *Layout of check-in areas, security, and gates*
- *Shops, eateries, and passenger facilities*
- *How travelers flow through different sections*

CHAPTER 6: SECURITY

- Screening of passengers and baggage
- Rules about liquids, sharp objects, and restricted items
- Advanced scanners and security checkpoints

CHAPTER 7: HOW BAGS ARE HANDLED

- Tagging and tracking luggage
- Conveyor belts, x-ray screening, and sorting systems
- What happens if bags are lost or delayed

CHAPTER 8: THE GATE

- Boarding passes, seating arrangements, and announcements
- Pre-boarding procedures for special needs
- Last-minute checks before takeoff

CHAPTER 9: THE PEOPLE WHO WORK AT AIRPORTS

- Airline staff, security officers, ground crew, and more
- How different teams coordinate to run daily operations
- Specialized roles that keep flights punctual

CHAPTER 10: THE GROUND CREW AND VEHICLES

- Baggage tractors, pushback tugs, and refueling trucks
- Loading and unloading processes on the apron
- Preparing planes for takeoff and arrival

CHAPTER 11: REPAIRS AND MAINTENANCE

- Upkeep of runways, terminals, and lighting systems
- Preventing and fixing wear and damage
- Scheduling repairs with minimal flight disruptions

CHAPTER 12: EATING AND SHOPPING AT THE AIRPORT

- Types of restaurants and shops
- Duty-free stores and common retail offerings
- How terminals cater to travelers' needs

CHAPTER 13: FIREFIGHTERS AT THE AIRPORT

- Why airports have their own firefighting teams
- Special trucks, foam, and training for aircraft fires
- Handling various emergencies on the airfield

CHAPTER 14: WEATHER: HOW IT AFFECTS FLYING

- Impact of fog, snow, wind, and storms on flights
- De-icing, runway clearing, and flight delays
- Forecasting and adjusting routes for safety

CHAPTER 15: MOVING GOODS BY AIR

- Air cargo operations and dedicated freighter planes
- Shipping perishables, high-value items, and mail
- Security, customs, and global trade

CHAPTER 16: HELPING PEOPLE WITH DIFFERENT NEEDS

- *Assistance for travelers with disabilities or special diets*
- *Family facilities, language support, and quiet spaces*
- *Staff training to provide inclusive service*

CHAPTER 17: NOISE AND AIRPORTS

- *How aircraft noise is measured and managed*
- *Community considerations and curfews*
- *Quieter engine designs and runway use*

CHAPTER 18: WAYS TO BE KINDER TO THE EARTH

- *Eco-friendly terminal designs and energy use*
- *Reducing emissions, waste, and water use*
- *Sustainable aviation fuels and green strategies*

CHAPTER 19: HANDLING EMERGENCIES

- *Airport firefighting, medical response, and evacuation plans*
- *In-flight and ground incidents, security threats, natural disasters*
- *Coordination among rescue teams, airlines, and control towers*

CHAPTER 20: THE NEXT STEPS FOR AIRPORTS

- *Future technologies: biometrics, AI, and eVTOLs*
- *Enhanced passenger comfort, faster security, greener operations*
- *Balancing growth, innovation, and community needs*

CHAPTER 1: A LOOK AT AIRPORTS

Airports are special places where airplanes take off and land. They are like big hubs that help people travel from one place to another by air. Many airports are huge, covering large areas of land. Some are smaller, with fewer flights each day. But all airports share the same purpose: they are designed to help airplanes operate in a safe and organized way. When you visit an airport, you will see many parts, like runways, terminals, gates, and towers. Each part has an important job. This chapter will explain what airports are, how they started, and why they are so important for air travel.

Air travel began more than a century ago, but in the early days, people did not have modern airports. Airplanes were smaller, and they did not need the big, long runways we see today. They could land on open fields. As airplanes became bigger, faster, and able to carry more people, we needed better places for them to land and take off. That is when the idea of an airport came about. Airplanes need lots of space to reach the right speed for takeoff and to slow down when they come back to the ground. Airports grew over time to meet these needs.

Airports usually have long strips of paved ground, called runways. They may also have large open areas where airplanes can move around before getting onto the runway. These areas are called taxiways and aprons. Taxiways are like roads for airplanes. They guide planes from where they park to the runway and back again. The apron is often where planes park, load and unload passengers, or refuel. All these features help airplanes move smoothly from the gate to the runway and then into the sky.

One key feature of an airport is the control tower. This tall building has windows all around, letting air traffic controllers look over the runways, taxiways, and other parts of the airport. Air traffic controllers use radios to talk with pilots. They tell pilots when to move, when to wait, and when to take off or land. This makes sure that there are no accidents and that every flight is timed correctly. The control tower is like the airport's eyes and ears.

Inside the airport terminal, you will find many different areas for passengers. There is a check-in area, where people drop off their bags and get their boarding passes. Then there is a security area, where you go through scanners to make sure everyone is safe. Past security, there are gates where people wait until it is time to board their plane. Some airports have many gates, each leading to planes going to different places. While waiting, people can walk around, buy food, or relax in seating areas. Large airports often have shops and restaurants too.

The airport terminal is designed to be a place where people can gather before they board their flight. It is important that the terminal is easy to use. Signs tell passengers where to go, such as which gate they need or where to find restrooms. In some airports, there are moving walkways and escalators to help people get from one part of the terminal to another more quickly. Some terminals even have special lounges where passengers can rest if they have long waits.

Airports also help the people who are passing through. For example, there may be an information desk where you can ask for help if you are lost or confused about your flight details. There might be airport staff walking around, ready to point you in the right direction. Many airports try to keep things clear, so you will see signs, screens with flight times, and announcements over loudspeakers.

Behind the scenes, airports are very busy. There is a lot of work that most passengers never see. People refuel airplanes, move bags from planes to baggage carousels, and load fresh meals onto flights. Workers drive special vehicles around, helping planes park and pushing them away from the gate before takeoff. These people keep the airport running well. Without them, there would be chaos.

A big part of an airport's job is handling a large number of airplanes each day. During busy periods, many flights might come in and out within a short time. When a plane lands, it needs to move off the runway quickly, so the next plane can land or take off. This requires great timing from air traffic controllers. They tell the pilot when it is safe to turn off the runway and onto a taxiway. Every minute matters.

An airport is also a place where safety is taken very seriously. From the security checkpoints to the way runways are arranged, everything is planned to reduce risks. Airports have firefighters ready in case of emergencies. They also have medical teams and special vehicles that can respond quickly if there is a problem. Everyone working in an airport trains to handle different situations.

One reason airports can handle so many flights is because they follow strict rules. These rules come from groups that oversee airplane safety around the world. They cover things like how often the runway lights are checked, how the ground crew guides planes, and when planes should take off or land. It might sound complicated, but these rules keep passengers and workers safe.

Another thing you will notice at big airports is the variety of airlines. Each airline has its own planes, staff, and ticket counters. Some airlines might focus on shorter flights within the same country, while others take people across oceans. Airports have to be ready for both kinds of flights. International airports have special places for customs and immigration. That is where people go to show their passports and declare any items they are bringing with them.

In addition to moving people, airports also handle cargo flights. Cargo planes carry goods of all kinds, from mail and packages to large parts of machinery. These goods often need to arrive quickly, and air transport is a fast option. Some airports have sections just for cargo, with warehouses and loading areas. This is different from where passenger planes park.

Even though airports are busy, they try to reduce the impact on surrounding areas. Planes can be noisy, and many airports follow rules to limit flights during certain hours. This helps people living near the airport get some rest at night. Some airports also watch how they use energy, aiming to reduce pollution. They might have recycling programs or use vehicles that run on cleaner fuel.

The size and shape of an airport depend on the needs of the city or area it serves. In some places, there might be only one runway. In big cities, you might find airports with multiple runways and several terminals. Very large airports sometimes have trains or buses to shuttle passengers between terminals. There can also be parking lots, car rental areas, and public transportation stations nearby.

A lot of planning goes into building an airport. Experts need to think about where the runways will go so that planes can take off and land safely. They also need to consider the wind and weather patterns, because planes usually take off and land into the wind for better control. Builders must clear enough space so that there are no tall buildings or trees blocking a plane's path.

Inside the airport, engineers and architects design the terminal so that it can handle crowds without becoming too cramped. They may add wide halls, many restrooms, and comfortable seating. The terminal needs to meet the requirements of security, baggage handling, and passenger services. Each new airport can take years of planning before it is ready.

For travelers, an airport might be the first place they get excited about flying. The sights and sounds are quite different from everyday life. Large windows let you see planes rolling by. There might be displays showing plane models or facts about aviation. Some airports have small museums, observation decks, or interactive exhibits. These can teach visitors about airplanes and the world of aviation.

Airports also adapt to new technology. In the past, people always had to check in at the airline desk, but now many airports have self-service kiosks. You can scan your ticket, get your boarding pass, and even print bag tags at these machines. Some airports use facial recognition gates for security or passport checks. Technology helps speed up processes and reduce waiting times, but staff are still around to help if there is a problem.

Another thing you will see at an airport is ground equipment. These are vehicles and machines that support flights. Baggage carts carry luggage to the airplane's cargo hold. Fuel trucks bring fuel for the planes. Catering trucks bring food and drinks. There are also tugs, which are small but strong vehicles that push or tow airplanes. Tugs help move planes without turning on the airplane's own engines while on the ground.

The airport's day usually starts early in the morning, when the first flights might depart. Some workers might have arrived even earlier to prepare everything. As the sun comes up, planes begin to take off in steady intervals. During the busiest times, you might see a line of planes waiting for their turn. The control tower makes sure that each plane follows its slot. Day or night, the airport keeps running. Pilots also rely on special runway lights when it is dark or foggy.

Weather can affect airports. If it is foggy, controllers might space out flights more. If there is a lot of snow, the airport has to clear the runway with plows and apply de-icing fluid to planes before they can take off. Storms can force planes to circle in the air or land at a different airport if conditions become unsafe. The airport plans for all these events to keep everyone secure.

Many people do not realize that airports have big teams maintaining the runways. The surface has to be kept in good condition with no large cracks or loose debris. If there is a small crack, it can grow bigger over time, creating a hazard for planes. So, maintenance crews often check the runways, lights, and signs to ensure everything is in good shape.

Behind the airport's walls, there might be offices for various operations. Airlines have staff who manage flight schedules and crew assignments. They make sure there is a pilot and attendants for each flight, and they track where each plane is at any given time. The airport authority manages the building, the property, and services like cleaning or snow removal. Some airports are so large that they are like small cities.

Airports are also places of connection. People from different countries pass through the same halls. You might hear many languages spoken around you. This is one reason airports often have signs using pictures or universal symbols. Even if someone cannot read a certain language, they can still figure out where to go by looking at the icons.

While airports are mainly about flights, some have attractions inside. For instance, an airport could have a play area for children, a small garden, or interesting artwork. Some airports are known for art displays or sculptures in their terminals. This can make waiting for a flight more pleasant. Sometimes, you can find large windows or balconies to watch planes land and take off.

The design and operation of airports keep changing as airplanes evolve. New airplanes might need different parking spaces or gates. Airlines might begin using new technology that changes the way passengers board. Airports must keep up to make sure they can support modern needs. This might mean building a larger terminal or adding new runways. Over time, an airport can expand to handle more and more travelers.

CHAPTER 2: WHY PLANES NEED AIRPORTS

Airplanes are wonderful machines that let us fly over great distances in much less time than it would take by car, train, or boat. However, airplanes cannot just land anywhere. They need a safe place to come down from the sky and to go back up. They also need people on the ground to guide them, handle their cargo, and make sure everything is working correctly. This is why airports exist. In this chapter, we will discuss all the reasons that airplanes depend on airports, from runways and support services to passenger facilities and safety rules.

One major reason planes need airports is because of runways. Airplanes are large and heavy, and they require long stretches of smooth surface to gain the speed needed for takeoff. They also need a clear space to land and slow down when they return to the ground. If a plane tried to land on a regular road or field, it could be very dangerous. The plane might run out of space to stop, or the surface might be uneven. Airports solve this problem by providing long, paved runways that are maintained and clear of obstacles.

Runways also have markings and lights that help pilots land and take off in the right spots, even when visibility is low. At night or during bad weather, runway lights guide pilots to the correct path. These lights and markings are carefully designed so that pilots know how much runway is left, when to slow down, and where to turn off once they have landed. This is very important for safety. It also helps air traffic controllers organize how planes use the runway.

Another vital reason planes need airports is air traffic control. The sky can get crowded, especially around busy airports. Planes also move very fast, so pilots need help to avoid getting too close to each other. Air traffic controllers give instructions to pilots about when to descend, when to line up for landing, and which runway to aim for. Without this coordination, airplanes might cross paths, which could be dangerous. The control tower is always checking weather reports, radar screens, and other data to direct planes in a safe and efficient way.

Communication is key. Pilots talk to air traffic controllers using radios. The controllers might say something like, "Flight 123, you are cleared to land on runway 27," which tells the pilot exactly where to go. The pilot responds to confirm they understand. Once the plane lands, ground controllers help direct the pilot to the correct taxiway and then to the gate. This system of guidance is only possible if there is an airport infrastructure in place.

Besides guiding planes, airports provide a place where planes can get all the services they need. For example, airplanes require fuel. At an airport, there are fuel trucks or fuel stations that bring the right type of aviation fuel to each plane. The fuel is stored in large tanks underneath the airport or near it. This is because planes can't just pull up to a regular gas station. They need specialized equipment and trained staff to handle jet fuel safely.

Airplanes also need regular maintenance. At many airports, there are maintenance hangars where technicians can repair or check different parts of the airplane. These hangars are large enough to fit entire planes inside. Technicians might change tires, inspect engines, or fix small issues that come up. Some airplanes need more detailed checks that can take days, or even weeks, to complete. Airports allow this work to happen in a controlled environment, with all the tools and parts nearby.

Another important service is baggage handling. When people fly, they bring suitcases, boxes, or other items. These bags need to be tagged, checked, and loaded onto the correct airplane. After the plane lands, the bags have to be taken off and sent to the baggage claim area so that passengers can pick them up. Airports have complex systems of conveyor belts and baggage carts to make sure items move to the right place. This process would not be possible if planes landed in random fields or roads.

Also, airplanes often carry cargo, such as mail, packages, or fresh produce. This cargo needs a secure place to be loaded and unloaded. Cargo staff use special vehicles and machines to lift heavy crates or containers onto the airplane. Some cargo is sensitive and must be stored at specific temperatures. Airports provide cold storage facilities and other resources to keep cargo in good condition before loading. They also have staff who check the cargo to make sure it matches the flight documents.

Security is another huge factor. Governments require that passengers and cargo go through checks before boarding a plane or being loaded. Airports have security checkpoints with scanners and guards. They also have rules about what items are allowed on a plane. If there were no airport, these checks would be much harder to do. By having a central location with secure entry points, airports help keep travelers and cargo safe.

Along with security, airports handle immigration and customs for international flights. When you fly to another country, you must show your passport and declare any items you are bringing. Officials at the airport check that you have the correct documents and that you follow the rules of the country you are entering. Without airports, there would be no simple way to track who is coming or going by plane.

Passengers also need a place to wait before boarding. Airports have terminals with seating areas, restrooms, shops, and food places. This helps make the waiting time more comfortable. People can find what they need, like a place to sit, eat, or charge their phone. The terminal is also where you get your boarding pass, drop off your bags, and pass through security. If planes did not have airports, passengers would not have a safe and organized place to gather before flights.

Weather can change quickly, and pilots need help dealing with it. Airports have weather stations that track conditions like wind speed, temperature, and air pressure. Pilots use this information to plan the flight path and make decisions about takeoff or landing. If the wind is too strong or the visibility is too poor, flights might be delayed or diverted. The airport also has equipment to clear snow and ice from runways, so planes can still operate during winter months. Without an airport's resources, dealing with weather issues would be risky.

Airports also provide a system of lights, signs, and signals so that planes can find their way around on the ground. An airplane's cockpit windows do not offer the best view of what is happening on the ground behind or beside the plane. Pilots rely on painted lines on taxiways, signboards with letters and numbers, and flashing lights to find the correct route to the runway or gate. Ground controllers might even give instructions like, "Turn left onto taxiway Bravo and hold short of runway 27," which means the pilot should stop before entering the runway area.

Apart from directing planes, airports have staff to direct ground traffic. Baggage carts, fuel trucks, and other vehicles must also follow specific paths and rules to avoid accidents. Some airports even have a separate ground traffic control system, ensuring vehicles do not cross paths with moving airplanes. This level of organization would be impossible without a dedicated place designed for airplane operations.

For long flights, airplanes need fresh meals, drinking water, and clean cabins. Airports have catering services that prepare meals and pack them on carts.

These carts are driven to the plane by catering trucks. The cabin of the plane might be cleaned after each flight, and the bathrooms are restocked with supplies. This level of service is possible because the airport has loading areas, staff, and vehicles to bring these items to the plane efficiently.

In the event of an emergency, airplanes rely on the airport's firefighting and rescue teams. Airports have specialized fire trucks that can spray water or foam to put out fires quickly. They also have ambulances and medical teams on standby. If a plane has trouble in the air, the pilot will often head to the nearest airport for help. The airport will be ready with trained teams who know how to handle aircraft emergencies. This can save lives and limit damage.

Airplanes need a certain kind of infrastructure around them to function correctly. Electricity is needed to power the lights and electronic systems on the ground. The airport provides places for planes to connect to external power while parked. Some planes can use their own power unit, but having a ground power option can be more efficient. Airports also have systems to remove waste from planes and refill clean water tanks. These kinds of services keep each airplane in good condition for the next flight.

It is not just the planes that benefit from an airport. Passengers, flight crews, and airline staff need places to work, rest, or organize tasks. Pilots might need a briefing room to review flight plans before takeoff. Flight attendants might check the supplies on board or learn about any special instructions for that flight. Airline managers keep track of flight schedules, seat reservations, and all the details that go into making sure travelers get to their destinations.

Without airports, airlines would have no base of operations. They might not know where to park their planes, where to board passengers, or how to manage regular checks. Airplanes cost a lot of money, and airlines need a secure place to keep them. Airports give them parking spots or hangars. Airports also generate income by charging airlines fees for using runways, gates, and other services. This system keeps the airport running and allows airlines to plan their finances.

Some might wonder: why can't planes land on water if they don't have an airport? In fact, some planes are designed to land on water (they are called seaplanes). But seaplanes are usually small and limited to certain conditions. Most commercial planes are not made to land on water. They need stable ground. Even if a plane is a seaplane, it still needs a proper docking area and a system to get passengers on and off. Airports (or seaports for planes) give structure and safety to these operations.

Airports also help coordinate air routes. When planes fly, they usually follow set paths in the sky. These paths help keep flights organized and avoid collisions. Most flights begin and end at airports, so the routes are planned accordingly. Airports exchange data with air traffic control centers, telling them the planes scheduled to depart or arrive. This information helps manage the airspace over large regions. Planes do not just float around at random; they move in a controlled environment.

For large cargo airlines, airports are crucial because they can schedule large planes to arrive at cargo terminals. Without an airport, shipping goods by plane in big amounts would be very difficult. The speed of air shipping is what makes it special. If there were no central place for loading and unloading, you could not move large quantities as easily. Many industries rely on quick air deliveries for urgent or expensive items. Hospitals sometimes need medical supplies flown in fast. Airports make this possible.

Finally, airports create a network of connections. By having airports in many places around the world, planes can link cities and countries that are far apart. People can travel for work, school, or to see family in distant places. Businesses can reach new markets, and mail can be sent rapidly. This network runs smoothly because each plane knows it can land at an airport prepared to handle it. Without these well-organized facilities, the idea of regular and safe air travel would fall apart.

CHAPTER 3: THE RUNWAY

A runway is a long, straight surface where airplanes lift off into the sky or come back down to land. It may look simple—just a big strip of pavement—but there is a lot of planning and science behind it. In this chapter, we will look at how runways are designed, why they need to be so long, what markings you can see on them, and how they help keep air travel safe.

The Shape and Length of Runways

Airplanes need a large amount of space to take off and land. The runway must be both long and wide. A plane needs to speed up to a certain rate before it can lift off the ground. It also needs enough room to slow down when it lands. Different types of planes require different runway lengths. For example, a small plane that carries only a few people needs less space than a huge jet that can carry hundreds of passengers.

Most big airports have runways that are thousands of feet long. Some of the longest runways can be more than two miles long. The width is also important, so the plane's wings and landing gear have enough space, and so that there is a bit of extra room in case the plane does not stay exactly in the center. The runway surface is made of strong materials, often concrete or asphalt, that can handle the weight of heavy airplanes.

Sometimes, an airport might have more than one runway. Having more than one allows planes to land and take off at the same time or in different directions, depending on the wind. In many cases, runways are built in different directions because wind patterns change. Planes take off and land better if they move into the wind. This gives them more lift and helps them slow down during landing.

How Runways Are Named

When you look at an airport map, you might notice that runways have numbers, like 09 or 27. These numbers come from the compass direction. A runway number is usually based on its heading, which is the direction it points on a compass, divided by 10. For example, a runway that points east (about 90 degrees) might be called Runway 09. If it points west (about 270 degrees), it might be called Runway 27. The same runway can have two numbers, one for each direction. If you land in one direction, you might be on Runway 09, but if you land the opposite way, you are on Runway 27.

Runway names help pilots and air traffic controllers know which runway they are talking about. If an airport has more than one runway pointing the same general direction, they might add a letter, like L for left, C for center, or R for right. This keeps everything clear. Pilots do not get confused about which runway they are cleared to use.

Markings and Lights on the Runway

Runways have many painted lines and symbols. These markings help pilots land in the right spot. They also show where the runway begins and ends. One important marking is the centerline, a white dashed line running down the middle. By following the centerline, the pilot can stay in the correct position during takeoff and landing.

Another marking is the threshold. This is the beginning of the part of the runway that is strong enough for landing. Often, you see broad white stripes near the runway's start. Planes aim to touch down within this area, not before it. Touching down too early could be dangerous because the surface before the threshold might not be made for the plane's weight.

There are also numbers painted on the runway, matching the runway's name. This helps pilots confirm they are using the correct one. You might also see special markings called touchdown zone markers. They look like pairs of white bars further down the runway, showing where the plane should ideally contact the ground for a safe landing.

Runway lights are crucial for flights at night or in poor weather. Along the sides, you will see white lights marking the runway edges. The centerline lights, if the airport has them, might be white, then change to alternating red and white near the far end, and finally solid red to warn the pilot that the runway is running out. There are also approach lights near the start of the runway, helping the pilot line up the plane during final approach.

Some airports have lights called PAPIs (Precision Approach Path Indicators). These lights help the pilot see if their path is too high, too low, or just right. They usually appear as a row of lights next to the runway. If the pilot is flying at the correct angle, they see two red lights and two white lights. If they see more red than white, they are too low; more white than red means they are too high.

Taxiways and Holding Areas

Connected to the runways are taxiways. These paths allow planes to move between the runway and other parts of the airport, such as gates, aprons, or hangars. Taxiways are usually marked with letters, like "Taxiway A" or "Taxiway B." Painted centerlines guide the pilot to stay in the correct lane. At night, blue lights often mark the edges of taxiways, and green lights mark the center.

Before a plane takes off, it might wait at a holding area near the runway. This spot is painted with a special hold short line. The pilot will stop and wait there until air traffic control says it is clear to move onto the runway. This prevents any risk of colliding with planes that are landing or taking off.

Why Planes Take Off and Land Into the Wind

You might have heard that planes like to face the wind when they take off and land. The main reason is that air moving against the plane's wings helps create lift. Lift is the force that makes an airplane rise into the air. By going into the wind, the plane does not need as much runway to get enough lift. For landing, facing into the wind helps slow the plane down. If the wind is behind the plane, it becomes harder to slow and might use more runway.

Most airports plan their runways based on the usual wind patterns in that region. If the wind changes, air traffic controllers might direct planes to use the runway that best faces the new wind direction. This switching of runway use can happen during the day, depending on shifting weather.

How Weather Affects Runways

Weather can greatly affect how a runway is used. If it snows, workers use plows and brushes to clear the snow off the runway. They might also spread chemicals to prevent ice from forming. If ice builds up, planes can skid when landing or taking off. Rain can also cause puddles. Designers often give runways a slight slope or grooves so water can drain away, reducing the risk of hydroplaning.

Strong crosswinds, which blow from the side, can be tricky. Pilots need special training to handle landings when the wind is not lined up with the runway. In some extreme cases, if the wind is too strong, planes might have to wait or land at a different airport. Fog can reduce visibility, making it harder for pilots to see the runway. Airports use special lights and instruments to help planes land safely in foggy weather, but sometimes visibility is so poor that it is not safe to land.

Runway Safety Areas

Runway safety is very important. Around the runway, there is often extra land called the runway safety area. This space is clear of buildings and other obstacles. It is there in case a plane goes off the runway surface by mistake. Having a clear area can reduce damage to the plane and keep passengers safer.

Airports sometimes have a special feature called an EMAS (Engineered Materials Arrestor System) at the end of the runway. EMAS is made of lightweight concrete or materials that crumble under the plane's weight, slowing it down quickly if it overruns the runway. This system can stop a plane without causing as much damage as a hard crash. It is especially useful at airports where there is not enough open land at the runway's end.

The Role of Ground Crew

The runway alone does not handle everything—people on the ground also play a key role. Ground crew members inspect the runway regularly. They check for cracks, debris, or damage that could cause a tire blowout. Even small objects, like bolts or stones, can be dangerous if a plane rolls over them at high speed. Crews also check the runway lights to make sure they are working, especially if the weather changes or if there has been heavy rain or snow.

If there is a problem on the runway, like an engine part falling off a plane, the air traffic control tower will close the runway. Then, ground crews will go out, remove the object, and check for damage. Once it is clear, the runway can reopen. This process may cause flight delays, but it is much safer than leaving debris that might lead to an accident.

Different Types of Runways

Not every runway is made of asphalt or concrete. Some smaller airports have grass or gravel runways, used mainly by small, light planes. These runways must still be well-maintained. Grass must be cut and cleared of any rocks. Gravel runways are common in remote areas, such as places with no paved roads or in regions with harsh weather. Pilots who use these runways have to be trained to handle the rougher surfaces.

You might also see water runways for seaplanes in certain parts of the world. However, these are quite different from land runways. Seaplanes need calm waters to land safely, and the pilot has to consider waves, tides, and other boats. Large commercial planes usually do not land on water except in emergencies, so most major airports have paved runways for jets.

Night Operations and Instrument Landings

Airports operate day and night, so runways need lighting and systems that guide planes in low visibility. One important system is called ILS (Instrument Landing System). This system has antennas near the runway that send signals to a plane's instruments. A plane equipped with ILS can follow these signals to land even if the pilot cannot see the runway well. This is critical during fog, rain, or snow.

Pilots trust the readings of their instruments to stay on the correct glide path and line up with the runway centerline. As they get closer, they might see the runway lights. If everything looks correct, they continue the landing. If something is off—maybe the wind is too strong, or visibility is worse than expected—they can perform a go-around. That means they power up the engines, climb back into the air, and try again or choose a different runway.

At night, runway lights become essential. The pilot can see the bright edge lights and approach lights. Some runways allow pilots to adjust the brightness of the lights by radio, especially at small airports without a full-time controller. This helps them see clearly without too much glare.

Upkeep and Inspection

Runways wear out over time because of the heavy weight of airplanes and the effects of weather. Airport maintenance teams watch for cracks and potholes. If they find small cracks, they seal them to prevent water from getting in and causing bigger damage. Sometimes, an airport must close a runway or part of it for repairs. Workers may resurface it with fresh asphalt or concrete, repaint the markings, and ensure the lights are in good shape.

The friction on the runway is also checked. When a plane lands, especially in wet conditions, it needs enough friction to brake and stop. If the runway is too smooth or covered with rubber from many landings, it can become slippery. In that case, workers might use special machines to remove built-up rubber or roughen the surface so planes can grip better during landing.

Declared Distances

Not all parts of the runway might be used for a plane's takeoff or landing roll. Airports sometimes list different lengths for takeoff, landing, accelerate-stop, and accelerate-go. These are called declared distances. A pilot needs to check these lengths to know if they have enough space for the plane's weight and the weather conditions. For example, if there is an obstacle like a hill or a building at one end, the usable distance for takeoff or landing might be shorter in that direction.

Runway Incursions

A runway incursion is when something—like another plane, a vehicle, or a person—enters the runway area without permission, creating a risk of collision. Airports work hard to prevent this. Signs and markings tell ground vehicles where they can and cannot go. Drivers at the airport must have special training and clearance from air traffic control to cross or drive near a runway. If an incursion happens, controllers may quickly direct any approaching plane to go around or switch runways to avoid an accident.

Sloped and Special Runways

Most runways look flat, but some have a slight slope if the land is uneven. In some mountainous areas, you might see runways with big slopes. Landing or taking off from these runways is more challenging. Pilots must be very careful with speed and approach because going uphill or downhill changes how the plane behaves. Some famous small airports in mountain regions have short, steep runways. Only experienced pilots can use them.

Another special case is runways near sea level that can be affected by tides or storms. In such places, designers must ensure that water does not flood the runway. Storm barriers or raised embankments might be used. If the runway floods, it can be out of service for hours or days until it is safe again.

Noise and Environmental Concerns

Large planes can be loud, and people living near an airport might be affected by the noise of takeoffs and landings. To help with this, airports often set up specific flight paths so that planes fly over less-populated areas when possible. Some airports have curfews or noise rules that restrict takeoffs or landings at night. Others plant trees or build noise walls. The shape of the runway approach paths can help reduce how much noise reaches homes.

Environmental rules can also affect the design of a runway. Builders might have to protect nearby wildlife or wetlands. They could create natural habitats in other areas to make up for building on open land. Airports might also look for ways to reduce pollution by using newer, cleaner materials or by limiting how long planes idle on the ground.

Technology in Modern Runways

Technology keeps changing the way runways operate. Some airports use advanced radar and sensor systems that track planes and vehicles. This helps air traffic controllers see exactly where each airplane is, even in poor visibility. In the future, there might be more use of lights that can switch colors, holographic signals, or other advanced tools to guide pilots on the ground.

Runway surfaces might also change over time. Engineers study new materials that are more resistant to wear or can handle extreme temperatures. Some runways have grooves or special coatings to improve traction and drain water. All these ideas aim to make taking off and landing safer.

Shared Runways with Military or Joint Use

A few airports share their runways with the military. In such cases, the runway might be used by both commercial flights and military jets. The airport must handle different types of traffic and follow both civil and military rules. Pilots might see military planes using separate taxiways or hangars. This arrangement can help a region save land and resources by having just one large airfield.

Human Factors in Runway Operations

Even though technology is helpful, people play a big role in making runways safe. Pilots must train for many hours to master takeoffs and landings. They learn about speeds, flap settings, and how to manage crosswinds. Air traffic controllers guide the planes, telling them when to enter the runway, when to wait, and when it is safe to take off or land.

Ground staff also need training. Someone who drives a fuel truck must know not to cross a runway without clearance. A maintenance worker must follow strict rules when painting markings or repairing lights, to avoid being on the runway when a plane needs it. All these people work together to prevent mistakes.

The Excitement of Watching Takeoffs and Landings

Some airports allow visitors to watch planes from observation decks or special areas. You can see the runway in action as planes line up, accelerate, and lift off the ground. You might also see planes touching down, tires smoking a bit as they contact the runway. It can be an exciting sight. People often enjoy seeing the power and skill involved in flight operations. Observing safely from a distance helps you appreciate just how important the runway is.

CHAPTER 4: THE CONTROL TOWER

Air travel involves guiding planes both on the ground and in the air. This guidance is the job of the control tower. You can often spot the tower because it is tall and has large windows at the top. From there, air traffic controllers watch and direct the movement of planes at the airport. In this chapter, we will talk about what the control tower does, how controllers communicate with pilots, the equipment they use, and why their work is so crucial for safe flying.

What Is the Control Tower?

The control tower is a building with a good view of the runways, taxiways, and apron. The top floor, often called the cab, has windows all around so controllers can see planes in every direction. Controllers also rely on radar screens, radios, and other tools to keep track of aircraft. The tower is the main point of contact for pilots when they are close to the airport—both approaching to land and preparing to take off.

While the tower is the most visible part of air traffic control, it is not the only part. Large airports have different control sections for ground movement, tower control, and approach or departure control. But in most cases, the word "tower" is used to mean the group of controllers who manage flights on and around the airport grounds.

Different Positions in the Control Tower

Inside the tower, you might find several controllers, each with a specific job:

- **Ground Controller:** This person manages planes and vehicles on the taxiways and other ground areas. They tell pilots which taxiway to use to get from the gate to the runway or vice versa. They also direct airport vehicles, like fuel trucks or maintenance cars, so they do not cross paths with planes.
- **Tower Controller (Local Controller):** This controller is in charge of planes on the runway and in the air near the airport. They give clearances for takeoff and landing. They watch the runways visually and on radar, making sure it is safe for a plane to enter or exit the runway.

- **Flight Data and Clearance Delivery:** At some airports, there is a person who handles flight plans and gives initial instructions to pilots before they start to taxi. This might be called "Clearance Delivery." They provide the pilot with a flight clearance, which includes the route the plane will fly and the altitude.
- **Approach/Departure Controller:** Not always in the tower itself but often in a nearby facility, this person handles planes that are arriving or leaving the airport's airspace. They use radar to line up incoming planes for landing and to direct outgoing planes away from the airport safely.

In smaller airports, one controller might handle multiple roles, especially if there is not much traffic. In bigger, busier airports, there can be many controllers, each focusing on one part of the operation to keep everything running smoothly.

Tools and Equipment in the Tower

The control tower uses a variety of tools:

- **Radios:** Controllers talk to pilots over assigned radio frequencies. Each pilot tunes their radio to the tower's frequency. When a controller wants to speak to a specific plane, they use the flight number. For example, "Flight 123, contact tower on frequency 118.3."
- **Radar Displays:** Some controllers have radar screens that show the position of each plane. They can track speed, altitude, and direction. In the tower cab, there may be a smaller radar display called a "tower radar" to see planes within a close range. However, the main approach radar might be located in a separate room or building.
- **Weather Instruments:** Controllers need weather data, like wind speed, wind direction, temperature, and visibility. Many airports have an Automated Weather Observing System (AWOS) or Automated Surface Observing System (ASOS). These sensors feed weather information to the tower, and the controller can share it with pilots.
- **Signal Lights:** If a plane's radio is not working, controllers can use colored light signals from the tower, like a green or red light, to instruct pilots to take off, land, or hold position. This is rare, but it is a backup method.
- **Flight Data Strips:** Some towers still use paper strips with flight information, such as the flight number, aircraft type, and planned route. Controllers move these strips around to track a flight's progress through

ground, tower, and departure control. Many places are switching to electronic systems, but paper strips are still common in some locations.

How Controllers Communicate

Communication between controllers and pilots must be clear and concise. They use a special phraseology to avoid confusion. For example, instead of saying "okay" or "got it," they say "roger" to mean they received the message. When controllers give an altitude or a heading, they use short, direct words. They also read back important instructions to confirm correctness.

An example of a takeoff clearance might be: "Flight 123, runway 09, cleared for takeoff." The pilot replies: "Cleared for takeoff, runway 09, Flight 123." This repetition helps both sides confirm they understand each other. If the pilot mishears, the controller can correct them right away. That prevents dangerous mistakes.

Controllers also talk to each other, especially when handing off a plane from one position to another. For instance, the ground controller might tell the tower controller, "Flight 123 is ready at runway 09," letting them know the plane is in position to take off. After takeoff, the tower controller might tell the pilot to switch to departure control, saying, "Contact departure on 124.7." Then the pilot changes the radio frequency and continues talking to the next controller.

Managing Takeoffs and Landings

One of the tower's biggest jobs is spacing out airplanes so they do not get too close. If a plane has just landed on the runway, the tower controller must make sure it has cleared the runway before allowing another plane to land or take off. This can be a challenge when the airport is very busy and flights arrive or depart only minutes apart.

The controller also looks out for wind direction and speed, making sure planes take off and land in the safest direction. If the wind changes, the controller might switch to a different runway or instruct planes to approach from the opposite end. They must keep track of any obstacles or other aircraft, such as smaller planes or helicopters that might fly at lower altitudes near the airport.

Handling Go-Arounds

A go-around is when a pilot decides not to land after beginning the approach. This might happen because the runway is not clear, the plane is too high or low on approach, or weather conditions are bad. Controllers quickly react to a go-around by giving instructions for the plane to climb away from the airport and join the traffic pattern again, or possibly try a different runway. The pilot might say, "Going around," and the tower responds with directions on heading and altitude. Timing is crucial, especially if there is another plane waiting to land or take off.

Keeping the Ground Organized

Ground movement can be chaotic if not well managed. At large airports, dozens of planes may be pushing back from gates, taxiing to runways, and rolling in from landings. The ground controller assigns each plane a path along the taxiways. They also separate airplanes from airport vehicles. Drivers who need to cross a taxiway must call the ground controller by radio. Only when the controller says it is safe can they proceed.

If two planes accidentally taxi toward each other on the same route, the ground controller must figure out who has the right-of-way and how to fix the conflict. This might involve telling one plane to stop and wait while the other passes. These instructions might sound like, "Flight 456, hold short of Taxiway Bravo," meaning do not cross the marking until cleared.

Weather and Traffic Flow

When storms, fog, or heavy winds occur, controllers must adjust the flow of traffic. They might slow down the rate of landings by placing planes in holding patterns above the airport. A holding pattern is a path in the sky where planes circle until the runway is free and conditions improve. Controllers must also watch for lightning, which can affect ground crews and fueling operations.

In snow or ice, controllers coordinate with snowplow teams. They might close one runway to allow workers to clear it, while using another runway for landings. If conditions become too dangerous, the airport may shut down operations temporarily. This is rare but happens if visibility is too low or the runway cannot be cleared of ice in time.

Emergencies

In an emergency, the control tower is the first to know. Pilots might report engine trouble, smoke in the cabin, or a medical problem. The tower controller notifies airport rescue and firefighting teams, who get ready for the plane's arrival. They might also give the plane priority to land, clearing other traffic out of the way. Quick communication is vital. The controller might say, "Flight 789, you are cleared to land any runway," meaning the pilot can choose whichever runway is easiest to reach.

If there is an accident on or near the runway, controllers stop all flights from landing or taking off until the runway is inspected and cleared. They may call in specialized vehicles to remove any debris or help injured passengers. Every moment matters in these situations, so controllers, ground crews, and emergency responders practice together to be prepared.

Technology and Automation

Modern control towers use computer systems to help track planes. Some airports use advanced radar that can even track planes and vehicles on the ground, called surface movement radar. This radar displays each moving object as a symbol on a screen. The controller can see the plane's call sign next to the symbol, so they know exactly where each flight is.

Data link systems allow controllers to send text-like messages directly to the cockpit, reducing the chance of misunderstandings over the radio. Pilots can read the instructions on a screen, acknowledge them, and follow them. Some airports are even testing remote towers, where controllers sit in a room far away. They watch a live video feed of the airport and have radar and weather data. This can help smaller airports where building a traditional tower might be expensive.

Daily Challenges in the Tower

Being an air traffic controller can be challenging. They must pay close attention to many details at once—weather, plane positions, runway conditions, flight schedules, and potential conflicts. They often work in shifts to stay alert. When traffic is heavy, they might handle dozens of planes in a short period, giving instructions quickly and accurately.

Controllers must also remain calm under stress. If something unexpected happens—a sudden change in wind, a pilot confusion, or an equipment problem—they have to solve it safely and quickly. Good teamwork is essential. Sometimes, a supervisor or another controller helps by taking over some tasks or assisting with certain flights.

Noise Management and Local Rules

Airports often have noise rules to protect nearby residents. The tower helps make sure planes follow these procedures, such as using a specific departure path that avoids dense neighborhoods. If an airport has a night curfew or limits on loud aircraft, controllers might schedule flights to meet those rules. They might also require planes to climb faster after takeoff to reduce noise. Controllers give heading or altitude instructions to meet these goals.

Special Flights and VIP Arrivals

Sometimes, airports handle special flights, like heads of state, government leaders, or important cargo. The control tower gets advance notice and plans carefully. They may give these flights priority or special security rules. They might block off certain taxiways or bring in extra security. Controllers coordinate with police, ground staff, and possibly military units if it is a high-profile arrival.

Training to Become a Controller

Working in a control tower requires training. People interested in this job often study aviation or take specific air traffic control courses. Then they go to a training center where they learn about rules, radar, weather, and radio phraseology. They practice in simulators that recreate busy airports. After passing exams, they might start as an assistant controller or apprentice at a smaller airport. Over time, they can move up to busier airports or more advanced roles.

Controllers have to pass medical and hearing tests because they need sharp eyesight and hearing to catch all details. They also must have good decision-making skills and the ability to stay calm when problems arise. Because they handle thousands of flights each day at busy airports, mistakes can have serious consequences. That is why the training is strict and why controllers often have limits on how long they can work without breaks.

Airport Coordination

The tower does not work alone. It communicates with other airport services:

- **Maintenance crews** tell the tower when they need to work on the runway or taxiways.
- **Fire and rescue teams** tell the tower when they are performing drills or training.
- **Ground services** let the tower know if they have special operations, like towing a plane across active taxiways.

All these teams share information so that the tower can plan the movement of planes around the airport without conflicts. If maintenance is happening on one taxiway, controllers route planes around it. If the runway is closed for inspection, no one lands or takes off until it is reopened. Good coordination helps keep operations safe and efficient.

Handling Different Aircraft Types

The control tower must handle different types of planes: large jets, small propeller planes, cargo planes, and helicopters. Each has different speeds and climbing or descending rates. A small plane moves slowly and might need more time on the runway. A large jet can take up most of the runway width. Helicopters might hover or fly in from a different angle. The tower controller adjusts spacing accordingly. For instance, if a small plane lands right after a large jet, it could experience turbulence called wake turbulence. Controllers keep a safe distance between planes to avoid these problems.

Coordinating with Nearby Airports

Large cities might have multiple airports close to each other. The control towers and approach control centers talk to each other to avoid sending planes into conflicting paths. If two airports are only a few miles apart, controllers carefully plan each plane's climb or descent to prevent them from crossing at the same altitude and location. This regional coordination is key to keeping everyone safe in busy airspace.

Future Developments in Air Traffic Control

As technology advances, control towers may see more automation. Artificial intelligence could help controllers by alerting them to possible conflicts or suggesting safe distances. Some airports already use digital towers with high-definition cameras and remote operations. This could allow one control center to serve multiple smaller airports, saving costs and improving coverage.

However, even with new technology, human controllers will still be needed. Their ability to make quick decisions, handle unusual events, and communicate clearly is hard to replace. In the future, we might see better tools and data systems that support their work, but the role of the human controller remains important.

Why the Tower Is So Important

Without the control tower, planes would have to guess when it was safe to take off or land. With many flights each day, that would be very risky. The tower's job is to keep flights organized and ensure no two planes use the same runway at the same time. They also keep ground vehicles away from moving aircraft. This level of coordination is what makes modern airports function smoothly.

When pilots arrive at an airport, they rely on the tower to give them landing clearance, wind information, and instructions on how to reach the gate. When they depart, the tower confirms the runway is free and that no other plane is on a collision path. The tower also reacts quickly to changing weather, emergencies, or other sudden events.

CHAPTER 5: THE TERMINAL

An airport terminal is the place where people go before and after they fly. It is a hub of activity, with many sections designed to handle different needs. In most cases, passengers begin their time at the airport in the terminal, and they also return to it when their flight is over. Although it might seem like just a big building, the terminal has many functions. This chapter looks at all the things you can find and do in an airport terminal, how it is set up, and why it is so important for smooth flying.

Arriving at the Airport

When people first get to the airport, they usually head toward the main doors of the terminal. Outside, there may be cars, buses, or trains dropping off passengers. The terminal entrance is often wide, with automatic doors and signs telling you where to go. Some airports have separate entrances for "Departures" and "Arrivals." Departures is for people who are getting ready to fly out. Arrivals is for people just getting off a plane.

Inside the terminal, you might see big screens showing flight times. These screens tell you which flights are scheduled, when they depart, and where to check in. They also show if a flight is on time, delayed, or canceled. Each flight is listed with a code that usually includes a combination of letters and numbers, like "AB123." The letters stand for the airline, while the numbers show which flight it is.

Check-In Counters

One of the first areas people visit is the check-in counter. Each airline has its own set of counters. Sometimes there are long lines, especially at busy times of day. You can walk up to the counter, give your name or reservation details, and show your ID. The airline staff will check your booking, print your boarding pass, and take any bags you want to put in the cargo hold. They put a tag on each bag to show where it is going. Then the bags go on a conveyor belt, disappearing behind the counter.

These check-in counters are designed to handle many passengers quickly. The staff must check that each person is on the correct flight and that their bags are within the allowed weight. They also make sure no forbidden items end up in the cargo hold. This process can be fast or slow, depending on how many travelers are flying that day. Some people choose to check in online before getting to the airport, which can save time. However, they still drop off their large bags at a special line called "Bag Drop," which works similarly to a normal check-in counter.

Self-Service Kiosks

In many modern terminals, you will see self-service kiosks near the check-in area. These are machines that let you check in by yourself. You might scan a barcode from your phone or type in your details. The kiosk will print your boarding pass and any tags you need for your bags. Then you can head to a bag drop counter to hand over your luggage. This helps you avoid the longer lines at the main counter.

Airlines and airports use these kiosks to speed things up. Fewer staff are needed at the counters, and passengers who already know how to check in can do it quickly on their own. Still, staff members stay nearby in case someone has trouble with the kiosk or needs help printing tags.

Special Check-In Areas

Some airlines offer separate check-in areas for certain passengers. For example, there might be a counter for people who need extra help, such as those using wheelchairs or those with small children. Sometimes, there is a separate area for travelers who fly very often with an airline. These passengers might have special membership cards that let them check in at a quieter desk. The idea is to make the airport process simpler for everyone, depending on their needs.

The Terminal Layout

Beyond the check-in area, you will likely see signs for different sections of the terminal. Big airports can have multiple levels. For instance, one level might be for check-in and security, while another level might be for gates and shops. Escalators, elevators, and stairs connect these levels, and there may be moving walkways in long hallways. These moving walkways look like flat escalators. They help you get from one end of the terminal to another more quickly.

You may also find places to sit down, sometimes with charging stations for phones or tablets. In large terminals, there can be entire seating sections to accommodate many people. Seats near big windows are popular because they let you watch planes take off and land. The terminal often has announcements about flights over loudspeakers, reminding you to go to your gate or letting you know about delays.

Security Checkpoints

After check-in, the next main step is going through security. We will look at this in more detail in the next chapter, but it is worth mentioning here because it is part of the terminal experience. You usually wait in line, show your boarding pass and ID, and place your carry-on items through scanners. Once you pass security, you enter the "secure" side of the terminal, where the gates and waiting areas are located.

Shops and Dining

Inside most terminals, especially the secure side, you will find shops that sell things like snacks, books, or headphones. There might be clothing stores, souvenir shops, or other small shops where you can browse while waiting for your flight. In some airports, there are large duty-free stores that sell items without certain taxes, but those are usually found in international terminals.

Dining options vary by airport. You might find fast-food outlets, coffee shops, or sit-down restaurants. Some travelers like to grab a quick snack before heading to the gate, while others prefer a full meal. Airports often try to provide various food choices, including healthier or vegetarian options. Eating areas usually have tables or counters where you can relax while waiting.

Waiting at the Gate

The gate is where you will board your plane. Gates are usually labeled with letters and numbers, like "Gate B10" or "Gate C22." The gate area will have rows of seats for passengers. Screens near the gate show the destination, boarding time, and flight number. Airline staff at the gate will scan boarding passes and let people on the plane when it is time. They might call passengers in groups, such as people who need extra help first, followed by those in the back rows of the plane, and so on.

If you arrive at your gate too early, you can sit, read, or watch the planes through the windows. You might want to double-check the departure screens to make sure there have been no last-minute changes. If a flight is late, gate agents might make announcements to let you know when they plan to start boarding.

Lounges

Some terminals have lounges run by airlines or special companies. These lounges are quieter spaces with more comfortable seating. They might serve drinks and small snacks. People who fly a lot with a certain airline or who have special memberships can use these lounges. Sometimes, you can pay for a one-time pass. Lounges can be helpful for passengers with long waiting times, as they can rest, use free Wi-Fi, and sometimes even take a shower, depending on the lounge.

Special Areas and Services

Terminals often offer additional services for passengers who need them. For instance, there might be a children's play area so kids can have fun while waiting. You might see a small clinic or first-aid station in case someone feels sick. Many airports also have a prayer or quiet room where people of all backgrounds can sit peacefully. Some terminals have business centers where you can use computers or printers.

There may also be currency exchange counters for those who need money in a different currency, along with banks or ATMs. In bigger airports, you might find a post office or mailing service. These extras aim to help travelers with anything they might need before or after flying.

Arrivals Area

When flights land, passengers walk off the plane into another section of the terminal. This could be the same physical area as the departure gates, or it might be a separate part of the building. Signs will direct arriving travelers toward baggage claim. Sometimes, if it is an international flight, passengers must go through immigration first. Then they head to a luggage carousel, which slowly spins while bags come out.

The arrivals area often has a waiting space for friends or family who have come to pick someone up. Some airports place the arrivals hall on a lower level, so you might have to take an escalator down. In many big terminals, you can see people standing by with signs or balloons, hoping to spot their arriving loved ones. Meanwhile, announcements play, saying which baggage carousel belongs to which flight.

Baggage Claim

One of the busiest sections for arrivals is baggage claim. A baggage carousel is like a moving belt in a loop. Airport workers unload suitcases from the plane onto the system behind the wall, and the bags come out on the carousel. You find a spot around it, watch for your bag, then pick it up. Big airports might have many carousels, each assigned to a different flight.

Sometimes, suitcases can get lost or delayed. If that happens, travelers go to the airline's lost baggage desk, usually located near the carousels. The staff there can help track where the luggage is. They might deliver it to your home or hotel if it arrives later. It is always a relief to see your bag on the carousel after a long flight!

Signs and Wayfinding

Terminals are designed with signs so people can find what they need. You will see arrows pointing to gates, baggage claim, restrooms, exits, and security. Some signs have pictures in case people do not read the local language. Digital screens or boards also show flight updates, gate changes, and general directions. In big terminals, you might see color-coded sections or big letters on the walls. All of these help reduce confusion.

In some airports, there are volunteer helpers or staff members walking around, ready to give directions. They might wear a vest or a badge to show they work for the airport. If you get lost or do not know where to go, they can point you the right way or answer questions about services in the terminal.

Moving Between Terminals

Large airports might have more than one terminal. Sometimes they are connected by walkways, trams, or shuttle buses. You might have to switch terminals if you have a connecting flight on a different airline. Signs will tell you how to get from Terminal 1 to Terminal 2, for example. If the terminals are far apart, there might be a free shuttle bus that stops every few minutes. It is wise to check your flight details to make sure you go to the correct terminal, so you do not run out of time.

Cleaning and Maintenance

Behind the scenes, a team of cleaners and maintenance staff keeps the terminal looking nice and functioning well. They vacuum floors, wipe seats, and clean restrooms. They pick up trash to keep the environment tidy. Maintenance workers also check escalators, lights, and electronic screens to ensure nothing is broken. The terminal needs to stay safe and welcoming for people, even during the busiest hours of the day.

In some areas, you might see machines scrubbing the floor at night or early in the morning. Windows facing the runway can get dirty from dust and rain, so window cleaners may be lifted in special platforms to keep them sparkling. Heating and cooling systems need regular checks, too, so that the temperature stays comfortable.

Lost and Found

If you misplace something in the terminal, there is usually a lost and found office. Airport staff collect items that get left behind and store them securely. If you realize you left your jacket or phone behind, you can go to the lost and found or call them later. It helps if you can describe the item clearly. They will check their collection to see if it matches what you lost. Airports often keep these items for a certain period before donating or discarding them if nobody claims them.

Information Desks

Terminals usually have an information desk or booth. Staff there can answer all sorts of questions. They can tell you where the nearest restroom is, how to find your gate, or the best way to get into the city once you leave the airport. They might also have maps or brochures about the airport. Some large airports have multiple information desks spread throughout the terminal. They can be a big help if you feel confused or if your flight changed gates and you are not sure where to go.

Keeping an Eye on Time

Airports run on tight schedules, so keeping track of time is important. Terminals display many clocks and flight screens. You might notice that the local time is always clearly shown. This helps travelers who come from other time zones. It is easy to lose track of time in a big terminal, especially if you stop for food or shopping. Flight announcements over the speakers often include reminders, like: "This is the final call for flight ABC123 to Gate D4." When you hear something like that, it means boarding is almost done.

Planning for Crowds

During busy seasons or holidays, terminals can get crowded. Airports plan for extra staff at check-in and security to manage longer lines. They might use rope barriers or signs to guide lines in a zigzag pattern, so people do not block hallways. Some airports open extra security lanes to speed up the process. Seating areas can fill up quickly when many flights leave around the same time.

If the terminal gets too full, staff may direct people to different sections where there is more space. In rare cases, if weather causes many canceled flights, some travelers might have to sleep in the terminal. Airports usually do their best to provide cots or a resting area, but it can still be uncomfortable. Terminals are meant for short stays, so overnight problems can be tough for passengers.

CHAPTER 6: SECURITY

Air travel is one of the safest ways to go from place to place, and a big reason for that is security. In an airport, security is not just about checking bags. It includes many systems, rules, and people who work together to make sure dangerous items or activities do not enter the airport or plane. This chapter explains how airport security works, the tools they use, and what you can expect when going through the checkpoint.

Why Airport Security Is Needed

Airplanes carry many passengers, and each has belongings in bags or backpacks. If someone were to bring dangerous items aboard, it could put everyone at risk. Airport security exists to prevent this. It also stops people who might want to break rules or cause harm. By screening everyone in a careful way, security officers greatly reduce the chance of a serious problem happening in the air or on the ground.

Security also checks that items placed in the cargo hold are safe. Some travelers might pack things that are not allowed on a plane. Rules exist for liquids, sharp objects, or anything that could start a fire. Airport security staff make sure these rules are followed. In addition, they watch out for suspicious behavior. If someone seems to be acting in a concerning way, security officers can ask questions or do a more detailed search.

The Security Checkpoint

The most familiar part of airport security is the checkpoint. This is where you line up to have your ID and boarding pass checked. Then you place your carry-on bags, coats, and other items in bins that go through an x-ray machine. You might also walk through a metal detector or a scanner. This process can feel routine, but it is carefully designed.

- **ID and Boarding Pass Check:** A security officer scans your boarding pass. They also check your ID or passport to confirm it is really you. This prevents anyone from using a stolen or fake boarding pass.
- **X-Ray Screening:** Your bags, including purses and jackets, go on a conveyor belt that passes through an x-ray machine. The x-ray gives

security officers a view of what is inside without opening the bag. They look for shapes of prohibited items, such as large knives or weapons.
- **Metal Detectors or Body Scanners:** You might walk through a metal detector that beeps if it senses metal on your body. Some airports use full-body scanners that use harmless waves to detect items under clothing. If the machine senses something, you might have a pat-down by an officer of the same gender.

If an officer sees something questionable on the x-ray screen, they will pull the bag aside for a closer look. They might open it and ask about specific objects. Sometimes, an officer will wipe the outside of a bag or item with a special swab, then test it for traces of explosives or other substances. These measures help keep everyone safe.

Rules About Liquids and Other Items

You may have heard about the liquid rule. Passengers are only allowed to bring a small amount of liquids, gels, or aerosols in their carry-on bags. Usually, each container must be 3.4 ounces (100 milliliters) or less, and all must fit in a clear plastic bag. This includes things like toothpaste, shampoo, or lotion. Larger containers must go in checked luggage instead. This rule was made to reduce the risk of harmful substances being brought onto the plane.

Sharp objects, like scissors or knives, can cause problems, so these are either banned or heavily restricted in carry-on bags. Some sports equipment, like baseball bats or hockey sticks, is also not allowed in the cabin. Security officers check for these items on the x-ray screen. If they find something that is not allowed, you might have to throw it away or place it in checked luggage (if you have enough time to go back to the check-in area).

Taking off Shoes and Other Steps

At some airports, passengers remove their shoes before going through the scanner. This is because shoes can hide items, or have metal parts that set off the detector. However, not all airports follow the same rule. In some places, only random checks or certain travelers are asked to remove shoes. Passengers might also need to remove laptops, tablets, or liquids from their bags and place them in separate bins. This makes it easier for the x-ray operator to see what is inside each item.

These steps can feel like a lot, but they speed up the screening by making images on the x-ray clearer. Security officers do not need to guess if something is hidden. It also prevents slowdowns when a bag has to be re-scanned multiple times. If you are ever confused about which items to remove, there are usually signs and staff to guide you.

Random Checks

Even if you follow all the rules, you might get selected for a random check. This means a security officer may swab your hands or open your bag for a closer look. They might ask you to step aside for a quick pat-down. These random checks help ensure nobody is singled out by appearance alone. They also make it harder for someone dangerous to guess how to slip through the system. Random checks are common in busy airports, so do not worry if it happens to you. It is just one more layer of safety.

Full-Body Scanners

Many airports now use full-body scanners instead of just metal detectors. These machines can find items that might not have metal in them, such as plastic or ceramic objects. The technology has changed a lot over the years. Early scanners sometimes showed a detailed image of the person's body, but newer machines usually show a generic outline and highlight areas of concern. If the scanner detects something unusual, security officers might do a pat-down to see what it is. They work to keep the process respectful. The goal is to ensure no dangerous objects slip through.

Baggage Screening for Checked Luggage

Not only do your carry-on bags go through scanners, but your checked luggage also gets screened after you drop it off at the airline desk. Most airports have big machines behind the scenes that x-ray or scan each suitcase. Some machines use advanced technology that can detect explosives or other risky items automatically. If a bag looks suspicious, security staff might open it for inspection. They usually place a note inside stating that your bag was opened for security reasons if you are not present.

These behind-the-scenes screenings help prevent threats from reaching the airplane's cargo hold. It also means that security can double-check items that might not have been allowed in the cabin. Sometimes, if you pack something unusual (like a special tool or device), it may trigger a closer inspection. That is why it helps to know your airline's rules about checked items before you pack.

Immigration and Passport Control

If you are flying internationally, you will go through immigration checks. This is where officers scan your passport, check your travel documents, and confirm you have the right to enter or leave a country. Sometimes this happens when you depart, other times when you arrive, or both. Immigration checkpoints are often separate from the regular security checkpoint. The officers there look at your passport, may ask about the purpose of your flight, and then stamp your passport if needed.

In some airports, security and immigration checks happen close together. In others, they happen in different areas. The main purpose of immigration checks is to control who enters or leaves a country. Security is more about what items and people are allowed on the plane. Both processes aim to keep everyone safe, but they focus on different details.

Customs Checks

When you arrive from another country, you may have to go through customs. Customs officers make sure you are not bringing illegal items, plants, or certain foods into the country. They also check if you need to pay taxes on goods you bought abroad. Some countries ask you to fill out a form stating what you are carrying. Others use an e-Gate system, where you scan your passport and declare items on a computer screen. If everything is normal, you can pass quickly. If the system flags something, a customs officer may inspect your luggage or ask more questions.

Airport Police and Security Officers

Beyond the checkpoint, airports also have officers who walk around the terminal and the outside areas. Some are airport police, while others are private security hired by the airport. They watch for anything suspicious, such as bags left alone or people acting strangely. In many airports, they have bomb-sniffing dogs or K-9 teams that can detect explosives by smelling them. You might see dogs and their handlers patrolling around. This is another layer of safety that often works quietly in the background.

Behavioral Detection

In some airports, security staff are trained to notice signs that a person might be hiding something. This is called behavioral detection. They watch how people move, whether they look unusually nervous, or if they avoid eye contact. While nervousness alone is not proof of wrongdoing, a combination of certain behaviors can make officers more cautious. If they suspect something, they might speak to the person or carry out extra screening. However, this method must be used carefully to avoid wrongly judging innocent travelers.

Keeping Lines Moving

One challenge in airport security is balancing safety with speed. Nobody likes long lines, and the security process can slow down if many flights depart around the same time. Airports plan how many checkpoints to open and how many officers to staff them. They also set up line dividers and signs to make the line flow smoothly. In some places, you can see digital boards showing wait times for each checkpoint. That way, travelers can pick the line that moves faster.

During very busy times, airports might encourage people to arrive earlier. They might add special lanes for families, people with special needs, or those without carry-on bags. These steps can help keep the line from getting too long. Security officers might also ask you to be ready: have your boarding pass out, remove items from your pockets, and take off jackets if required. Doing this can speed things up and make the process easier for everyone.

Trusted Traveler Programs

Some countries have "trusted traveler" or "pre-check" programs. People who join these programs go through a background check beforehand. Once approved, they can often use a special lane at security. In these lanes, travelers might not need to remove their shoes or jackets, and laptops can stay in bags. This helps move them through faster. The idea is that these passengers are considered lower risk, so they do not need the same level of screening every time.

Technology Behind the Scenes

Airport security is not only about the machines you see at the checkpoint. There is also technology that scans passenger names against watchlists, checks for stolen passports, and flags unusual booking patterns. If someone with a suspicious history buys a plane ticket, security agencies might be alerted. Many airports also use advanced cameras all around the terminal. These cameras are monitored by security staff who can quickly see if there is a problem.

Some new systems are being tested to make security faster and safer at the same time. For example, there are new x-ray machines that give a 3D image of bags, letting officers see inside more clearly. Automated lanes let multiple passengers load trays at once, speeding up the line. As technology improves, airports continue to upgrade their security setups.

Training Security Officers

Security officers receive detailed training before they begin working. They learn how to operate x-ray machines, how to spot suspicious shapes, and how to search bags if something looks odd. They also learn how to handle different situations, such as finding a prohibited item. Part of the training involves dealing calmly with upset or stressed travelers. Officers must follow strict rules to respect personal privacy and avoid profiling.

In some places, officers take regular tests to prove they can still recognize dangerous items on the x-ray screen. This keeps their skills sharp. If an officer fails a test, they might get extra training until they improve. Since the security environment changes over time, airports update their training to cover new types of threats or updated technology.

What Happens If You Break the Rules

If someone tries to bring a banned item through security, the consequences depend on what the item is and why they have it. If it is simply an oversized bottle of shampoo, security might just throw it away. If it is a serious weapon, like a gun or a large knife, the person could be stopped and questioned by the police. In the worst cases, there can be arrests or fines. This is why it is so important to check the rules before packing.

If you accidentally leave liquids in your bag and the officer catches it, they may give you the chance to discard the items or place them in checked baggage (if you have time). But if you continue to violate the rules, you could miss your flight or face penalties. Always pay attention to the instructions on signs and from officers.

Handling Emergencies

Security also prepares for emergency situations. If there is an alarm for fire, security officers may help direct people to exits. If a suspicious bag is found, they might clear an area and call the bomb squad. If someone becomes threatening, airport police step in. Drills and practice sessions help everyone know what to do. These drills include scenarios like evacuations, lost children, or medical emergencies. The main goal is to keep people safe and calm.

Future Security Methods

As new technology develops, airports look for ways to make security even better. Some are testing scanners that can inspect liquids without opening them, so you would not have to remove anything from your bag. Others are exploring facial recognition systems to match travelers with their passport photos automatically. While these systems can speed up lines, they raise questions about privacy. Airports have to balance the benefits of faster, more effective checks with the need to protect personal information.

Robots or automated drones might be used in the future to patrol the terminal. These machines can scan for unusual activity and report back to a control center. Improvements in AI may help spot odd patterns in passenger movement. Still, no matter how advanced the machines get, humans will likely remain involved. Security officers make judgment calls that a machine cannot always match.

Tips for Going Through Security Smoothly

Even though we do not want to repeat advice from earlier chapters, here are a few ideas specific to the security process that can help:

- **Pack Properly:** Keep liquids in small containers if you plan to carry them on. Place them in a clear plastic bag on top of your belongings so you can remove them easily.
- **Organize Your Electronics:** If the airport requires it, place laptops and tablets in a separate bin. That way, you do not have to rummage through your bag at the last minute.
- **Check Rules in Advance:** Different airports or countries have different guidelines. If you are unsure, look up the rules for your airline and destination.
- **Follow Instructions:** Listen to security officers. If they say to remove your shoes or raise your arms in a scanner, do so promptly. Politeness and cooperation usually make things go faster.
- **Be Aware of Prohibited Items:** Know what objects are not allowed in carry-on bags (like large knives or fireworks) so you do not have to discard them at the checkpoint.

These points help the line move more smoothly and reduce stress for both you and the officers.

CHAPTER 7: HOW BAGS ARE HANDLED

When people travel by plane, they often bring suitcases, backpacks, and other items. But how do all these items get from the check-in counter to the airplane? And after landing, how do they return to the correct passengers? The answer is a complex system of conveyor belts, scanning machines, baggage carts, and careful planning. This chapter explains each step in the path your bag takes, from the moment you hand it over at the airport until you pick it up at your destination.

Bag Drop and Tagging

It all starts when you arrive at the check-in counter (or use a self-service kiosk, then visit the bag drop). The airline staff weighs each suitcase to ensure it does not go over the allowed limit. They also attach a tag, which is often a long sticker with a barcode or QR code. This code holds details like your flight number and final destination. Each piece of luggage usually gets its own unique code, so the system can identify it later.

Sometimes, you may have more than one flight on your trip. In these cases, the staff might print a tag that shows all stops, so your bag can be transferred automatically at connecting airports. If you are flying internationally, the staff might ask questions about what is inside your bag, making sure there are no restricted items. Once the bag is tagged, they place it on a conveyor belt, and it disappears behind a curtain or a wall. Many travelers do not see what happens next.

Behind the Scenes: Conveyor Systems

Behind that wall is a network of conveyor belts that guide suitcases through the airport. Think of it like a maze, but controlled by computers and sensors. Each bag's barcode is scanned at various points. When the system reads the code, it knows which flight the bag should go on. As a result, the conveyors can direct the item along the correct path. If the bag needs to go to Flight 123, the belt might split at a junction, sending the suitcase down one route rather than another.

These belts are fast. Some airports move bags at speeds of several feet per second. Different airports use different methods. Some have a mix of conveyor belts and destination-coded vehicles (small carts on tracks). Others have tilt-tray sorters that pick up each bag and drop it onto another belt based on its destination. No matter the method, the goal is to sort and group bags for each flight.

Security Screening for Checked Bags

Before a bag is cleared to go onto the airplane, it passes through security checks. We learned in an earlier chapter about security for carry-on items, but there is also security for checked luggage. Large machines scan each suitcase, checking for anything that could be unsafe. These machines might use x-rays, explosive detection technology, or advanced imaging.

If the system flags a bag as suspicious, it is diverted off the main conveyor to a separate area. Security officers can open it for a closer inspection. They might look for items like flammable products, prohibited tools, or anything that could break airline rules. If they find a banned object, they may remove it, label it, or contact the passenger if needed. In most cases, everything is fine, and the bag continues on its way.

Loading Bags into Containers or Carts

Once a bag is cleared, it arrives at the section of the airport where ramp workers handle luggage. At many big airports, workers pack bags into special containers shaped to fit the airplane's cargo hold. These containers, often called Unit Load Devices (ULDs), can be metal or sturdy plastic and come in different sizes. Each container might hold dozens of suitcases. The workers stack them carefully, trying to use all the space without crushing fragile items. If the bag is going on a narrow-body plane (one aisle), they might load them directly onto baggage carts or larger containers that slide into the belly of the plane.

Ramp workers use scanners to read the tags again, confirming which flight each bag belongs to. If a bag is scanned and does not match the flight, the worker sets it aside to figure out its correct destination. This step helps prevent bags from going to the wrong place. Each container or cart is also labeled with the flight details, so staff know exactly where it must go on the airport tarmac.

Moving Luggage to the Plane

After packing the containers, workers use vehicles called baggage tractors or tugs to pull them across the airport ramp. You might see small trains of carts moving behind these tugs. Each cart has a metal or canvas cover to protect suitcases from bad weather. If the airport is busy, you will notice many tugs zipping around, taking bags to different gates. The drivers follow strict routes and must get clearance to cross active taxiways.

When they reach the plane, the containers or carts are placed near the cargo hold doors. Sometimes, a belt loader is parked at the plane's belly, allowing workers to move suitcases one by one up the conveyor belt. At other times, a special loader lifts entire containers into the hold. The process depends on the type of aircraft and the airport's equipment. Workers inside the cargo hold arrange the bags so they are secure and do not move around during flight.

Balancing the Weight

Planes need proper balance to fly safely. Too much weight in the back or front can cause problems. Airlines use a system called Weight and Balance to ensure the plane is loaded correctly. The baggage handlers and airline planners decide how many bags go in each cargo hold section. They might place heavier suitcases closer to the center of the plane. Meanwhile, lighter bags might go toward the ends. The load plan includes details like how many passengers are seated in each section of the cabin and the weight of any cargo or mail on board.

The pilot or flight dispatcher reviews a final load sheet before takeoff. This sheet shows the total weight and the distribution. If the plane is too heavy, ground staff might need to remove some bags or cargo. If the flight is not full, they can spread the weight out for better balance. This careful planning is one reason planes are so safe, even when carrying hundreds of people and their belongings.

Bags During the Flight

Once the plane takes off, luggage rides along in the lower part of the aircraft. There is usually no direct access to the bags from the passenger cabin, except on some small planes. The cargo hold is often temperature-controlled and pressurized if needed, especially when transporting animals or items that must stay above freezing. However, it might be a bit cooler and darker in the cargo hold than in the cabin.

If the flight has connections, the bags will need to be offloaded at the next airport. In many cases, the passenger never sees this process. They simply change planes or remain seated if continuing on the same aircraft. Meanwhile, ground crews quickly unload, sort, and reload the luggage that is supposed to travel onward.

Arrival and Offloading

When the plane lands and reaches the gate, ramp workers move into position. They attach a belt loader or a container loader to the plane's cargo hold. Bags are taken out in an organized way. If the plane will continue to another city with some passengers staying on board, handlers only remove the items that belong to the people disembarking at that airport.

For flights ending at that airport, all baggage is offloaded onto carts or containers. The ground crew scans each bag's tag again, confirming it has arrived. Then they take the items to the baggage sorting area in the arrivals section of the airport. From there, the luggage is placed on carousels for passengers to claim. You see these carousels in the baggage claim area, typically a big oval conveyor belt circling around. As the bags come out, you look for your suitcase and pick it up.

Transfers and Connecting Flights

Many trips involve a connection at another airport. In that case, your bag might not be returned to you in the middle of your trip (unless you have to clear customs). Instead, the airport staff takes it from your arriving plane, sorts it again, and then sends it to the next flight. This can be tricky if you have a short layover. That is why airlines try to keep track of where each bag is in the system. If there is a delay and you miss your connection, the airline might need to remove your luggage from the plane you were originally scheduled to catch.

Large airports have special baggage transfer facilities. Bags coming off one flight are quickly grouped by the next flight number. If the window for the connection is very short, staff might do an "express transfer" with those bags, rushing them to the next plane. If there is a mistake, a bag can end up on the wrong flight, which leads to missing luggage and extra work to reunite it with its owner.

Lost and Delayed Bags

Despite all the systems and checks, luggage can still go missing. Sometimes a tag falls off, or the bag is scanned incorrectly. Other times, the passenger switches flights at the last minute, but the bag does not get the updated details in time. If your suitcase does not show up on the carousel, the airline has a baggage service counter to help you file a report.

Airlines use software to track lost bags. They can search by description, flight routes, and even by partial tag numbers. Many times, the bag simply took a later flight or got stuck in sorting. In these cases, it arrives within a day or two. If a suitcase is truly lost, the airline may compensate the passenger according to the rules in that region. It can be frustrating, but this is why labeling your bag with your name and contact info is always a smart idea.

Oversized and Special Bags

Some items do not fit in a normal suitcase or weigh more than the standard limit. These might include sports equipment, musical instruments, or large strollers. Airports have special procedures for these. For instance, you might bring a surfboard or a bicycle. The check-in staff prints a tag just like any other item, but they often direct you to an oversized baggage drop. This area has conveyor belts or doors wider than the usual slots.

Because these objects can have irregular shapes, they go through special x-ray machines and might need extra handling. The airline might charge additional fees for items exceeding certain dimensions or weights. The workers who handle them must be careful to avoid damage. At the other end, these items sometimes appear in a special pick-up area, not on the regular carousel.

Priority Baggage

Some airlines offer priority baggage for passengers traveling in premium classes or who have higher membership status in a frequent flyer program. These bags are labeled with a special tag, often a brightly colored one saying "Priority." The idea is to load them last into the cargo hold so they can be taken off first. That way, these travelers can get their suitcases sooner at the destination.

In theory, priority-tagged luggage should appear before regular bags on the carousel. However, this does not always happen perfectly, because ground crews might need to move quickly and cannot always separate every item precisely. Still, the system attempts to give those bags a faster route.

Keeping Luggage Safe

Airlines and airports take security seriously, but incidents can happen. Bags might be tampered with, or items inside could break if not packed properly. For valuable or fragile items, many people use extra locks or place them in carry-on if possible. When checking a bag, it is wise to use sturdy luggage that can handle rough treatment, because conveyor belts and sorting machines can jostle it. Airport staff do their best, but with thousands of items moving through each day, some turbulence is expected for your suitcase.

Some travelers wrap their bags in protective plastic. Others prefer hard-shell suitcases. Most airports have CCTV cameras monitoring baggage areas, and staff members receive training to reduce the chance of theft. If you notice damage or missing belongings, you should report it immediately to the airline. They might help with repairs or compensation, depending on the situation.

Smart Luggage and Tracking

In recent years, new technology has appeared in the world of luggage. Some suitcases come with built-in GPS or Bluetooth trackers, letting you see where your bag is through an app. Others have electronic tags that automatically update with your flight info. However, certain rules apply about batteries in checked bags. If your bag has a non-removable battery, you might need to remove it or place the bag in carry-on. Always check the airline's guidelines.

Some airports are also testing better bag tracking through RFID (radio-frequency identification). When a bag with an RFID-enabled tag passes by a reader, it updates a database in real time. This can reduce errors, because scanning is automatic rather than a human or optical scanner needing a direct line of sight. As more airports adopt RFID, lost luggage rates could drop even further.

Baggage Storage at Airports

Sometimes, you might have a long gap before your next flight or want to explore a city without dragging your suitcase. Many airports offer baggage storage or lockers. You can drop your items at a desk or put them in a locker (paying a fee based on the number of hours). That way, you can walk around more freely. When you return, you show your ticket or receipt and retrieve your items. These facilities can also help if you arrive early and cannot check in your bags for another few hours.

Baggage Carousels and Claims

When you finally walk to baggage claim after your flight, you see large screens telling you which carousel to go to. This area can be busy, especially if multiple flights arrive at once. The bags come out in batches, usually from the plane that landed first. Workers in a secure area behind the wall place the suitcases onto the rotating belt. If you notice many identical suitcases, it helps to have a color ribbon or tag on yours. That way, you can spot it easily.

The airport might have multiple carousels for different flights. If you do not see your bag after all items from your flight seem to have arrived, you should visit the airline's baggage counter. There might be a delay, or your luggage could show up on a different carousel by mistake. Being patient is key, though it can be hard after a long flight.

Claim Checks and Controls

In some places, an airport employee or security officer might check that the tag on your bag matches the claim ticket you received at check-in. This prevents someone else from taking your suitcase by error or on purpose. These checks are common in airports where bags move through smaller areas, but not all airports have them. If you ever grab the wrong bag by accident, return it right away or contact the airline to fix the mix-up.

International Arrivals and Customs

On international flights, you usually get your checked bags before customs. You pick up your suitcase from the carousel, then walk through the customs area where officers might inspect your belongings or ask about items you are bringing into the country. If you have nothing special to declare, you might walk straight out. Otherwise, you go to a declaration line. Once you finish, you can exit and head to your next flight or go home.

In some airports, you recheck your bag right after customs if you have a connecting flight. That means you drop it at a transfer counter or place it on another conveyor belt so it can go to the next plane. This procedure ensures that you clear customs in the first country where you land, then continue your trip without needing to carry your luggage around the airport.

Handling Animal Travel

Sometimes, people fly with pets or other animals. The process for these animals can be more involved. If they are traveling in the cargo hold, staff must load them carefully into crates. These crates often have water bowls, padding, and enough space for the animal to move a bit. When the plane lands, ground workers try to offload these crates first so the animals do not stay in the hold too long. If the animal is going through a special service, it might be delivered to a separate area where the owner can pick it up.

Airports have rules about which animals can travel and how. Many require health certificates or vaccines. Some countries have quarantine laws. This means the animal may have to stay in a government-approved facility for a time. Though this does not directly involve standard baggage, it is still part of the airport's system of handling cargo and keeping living beings safe.

CHAPTER 8: THE GATE

Once your luggage is checked in and you have passed security, it is time to head to your gate. The gate area is where you wait to board the plane and where airline staff manage the final steps before takeoff. Though it might seem like a simple spot with seats and a door, a lot happens at the gate to get everyone ready to fly. This chapter explains the people, procedures, and systems involved in guiding you from the terminal waiting area onto your airplane.

Locating Your Gate

When you leave security, you are usually on the "airside" of the airport. That is the secure zone with duty-free shops, food places, restrooms, and most importantly, the gates. Each gate is labeled, often with letters and numbers, such as Gate A12 or Gate C9. Large airports can have many gates spread across different concourses. Monitors or signs help you find which concourse or wing you need. If you are unsure, staff at information desks can point you in the right direction.

Airlines list your gate number on the departure screens, along with your flight time and destination. However, gates can change unexpectedly. If the airline decides another gate is better, you might hear an announcement or see it on a screen that your flight has moved from Gate B15 to Gate B19. To avoid confusion, keep an eye on those monitors.

The Gate Area

When you arrive at the gate, you will see rows of chairs for passengers to sit. There may be charging stations or tables. Some gates have large windows overlooking the ramp, giving a view of planes parking. You might see ground crews loading bags, fueling the jet, or preparing the aircraft for departure.

A counter or desk at the front is where gate agents work. They have computers to check passenger lists, print extra boarding passes, or handle seat changes. Often, the gate area has a display screen showing the flight number, departure time, and destination city. Sometimes, it also shows the boarding group numbers or rows that will board first.

Boarding Passes and Seat Assignments

If you did not print your boarding pass at home or at check-in, you might do so at the gate. You hand your ID to the gate agent, and they will print a pass showing your seat number, boarding group, and any other details. If you have an electronic boarding pass on your phone, the gate staff can scan it directly from your screen.

Seat assignments are decided either when you booked the flight, checked in online, or visited the airline counter. If you want to change your seat, you can ask the agent at the gate, but options may be limited. Some airlines let you pay to upgrade to a better seat, while others might move you for operational reasons, such as balancing the plane or accommodating families who need to sit together.

Waiting for Boarding

Airlines schedule a specific boarding time, often 30 minutes to an hour before the departure time (this can vary by airline and flight length). While you wait, you can use restrooms, grab a snack, or charge your device. It is a good idea to stay near the gate, especially if your flight might start boarding earlier than planned. Airlines aim to board everyone and close the airplane door a bit before the departure time, so the plane can leave on schedule.

Gate agents sometimes make announcements. They might say there is a slight delay due to a late-arriving aircraft or explain the boarding groups. If you have questions—like if you need a seat for a child's car seat or if you have reduced mobility—you can talk to the gate agent. They can note any special arrangements in the computer system.

Pre-Boarding and Priority Boarding

Boarding usually happens in groups. First, passengers who need extra time or help, such as those in wheelchairs or families with small kids, are allowed to board. This is called pre-boarding. They can go ahead of everyone else, so they have time to navigate the aisle and get settled.

After that, airlines often board premium customers or frequent flyers. Sometimes they board by seat rows, like "rows 20–30" first, then "rows 10–19." Others have zones or group numbers printed on the boarding pass. For example, group 1 might go first, then group 2, and so on. This process helps organize the line, so people in the back of the plane get on before those seated up front. It can reduce congestion in the aisle and speed up boarding.

The Boarding Pass Scan

When your group is called, you line up at the gate door or the agent's desk. The agent scans your boarding pass. This scan updates the airline's computer system, letting them know you have officially boarded. If you have an e-boarding pass on your phone, you hold it up to a scanner. If you have a paper pass, you hand it to the agent, who either scans it or tears off a portion.

Sometimes, the system might beep to signal an issue. This could mean your seat changed, your pass needs reprinting, or there is a note on your reservation. The agent will resolve the problem quickly if possible. In some cases, they might ask you to step aside while they figure it out. Once everything is fine, you get the go-ahead to walk onto the jet bridge or down the steps leading to the plane.

Jet Bridges and Boarding Methods

At most large airports, gates connect to the aircraft using a jet bridge (also called a jetway). This is a movable walkway that lines up with the airplane door. You do not feel the elements outside, because the bridge is enclosed. The gate staff can adjust it up or down to fit different aircraft door heights. When you step through, you are effectively leaving the terminal and entering the plane.

Some airports, especially smaller ones, might not have jet bridges. Instead, you walk on the tarmac and climb airstairs or a small set of steps that are wheeled to the plane. In rainy or snowy weather, staff might provide umbrellas or place a canopy over the steps. Airports that handle wide-body jets often have two or more jet bridges, so passengers can board through the front and back doors at the same time. This speeds things up for large planes.

Carry-On Bags and Overhead Bins

As you enter the airplane, you see rows of seats, overhead compartments, and possibly flight attendants greeting you. If you brought a carry-on bag, look for space in the overhead bin near your seat. Larger bags might not fit if the plane is small or if the bins are already full. In that case, a flight attendant might tag your bag and place it in the cargo hold, returning it to you either at the gate after landing or at baggage claim.

Airlines have size limits for carry-ons. If your bag does not meet these limits, you might be asked to check it at the gate. This can happen when a flight is very full, and overhead space is limited. Gate-checking is often free, but it means you will have to pick up your bag at baggage claim later (or sometimes plane-side, depending on the airline).

Boarding Pass Checks on the Plane

Flight attendants might glance at your boarding pass to help you find the correct row. They want to make sure everyone sits in the right seat. If you have trouble locating your seat or stowing your luggage, they can assist. Once you sit down, be aware of instructions about seat belts, seatback positions, and electronic devices. The goal is to be ready for a timely departure.

Gate Announcements and Last Calls

Back at the gate, the agents continue to make announcements until everyone has boarded. They might call out passenger names if someone has not shown up. For example, "Final call for Passenger Smith, please proceed to Gate C5." This is your cue if you are in a nearby shop or restroom. If there is no response, the airline might remove that passenger's checked bags from the plane for safety, in case the person decided not to fly. That process can delay departure, so airlines try hard to get everyone on board.

Overbooked Flights and Volunteers

Sometimes, airlines sell more tickets than there are seats. This is called overbooking. If too many passengers arrive, the gate agent might ask for volunteers to switch to a later flight in exchange for compensation, like travel vouchers or meal credits. If not enough people volunteer, the airline can deny boarding to some travelers. They usually select those who checked in last, but the rules can vary. This is a stressful part of gate operations, and agents try to solve it fairly and politely.

Gate Upgrades and Standby Lists

Another important gate function is handling standby passengers or those hoping for an upgrade. If you are on standby, it means you do not have a confirmed seat yet. Gate agents will wait until most confirmed passengers have boarded. Then, if there is space left, they might call standby names and assign them seats. For upgrades, some passengers with frequent flyer status might be automatically upgraded if seats are available in a higher class. The gate agent sees a list on the computer and can clear these upgrades last-minute.

Assisting Passengers with Special Needs

Airlines aim to help passengers who have mobility challenges, hearing or vision differences, or other needs. This often happens at the gate. For example, if you use a wheelchair, staff can bring an aisle chair to help you board the plane, since the aisles are narrow. If you have a service animal, gate agents confirm the required paperwork or seating arrangement so the animal can fit safely. The agent might also arrange seating near an exit or the front row if it helps with easier entry and exit.

Coordination with Cabin Crew and Pilots

Gate agents do not work alone. They stay in contact with flight attendants and pilots about any important changes. For instance, if a passenger has a peanut allergy, they might inform the flight attendants so they avoid handing out peanut snacks. Or if there is a maintenance delay, the pilot can inform the agent, who then passes the information to passengers.

Pilots also need final counts: how many passengers are on board, how many bags there are, and how much cargo is loaded. The gate agent will close the flight in the computer system, providing the final passenger list. This data goes into the plane's load sheet, so the pilot and dispatch team can see if the plane's weight distribution is as planned.

Gate Closes and Pushback

Not long before departure, the gate agent will announce the gate is closing. This means boarding is done, and any latecomers risk missing the flight. The jet bridge door is locked, and the agent prints final paperwork. The pilot or ramp crew then prepares for pushback, which is when a tug pushes the airplane away from the gate. The seat belt sign is on, and everyone on board is expected to be seated.

From the passenger's perspective, this is the point of no return. If you arrive at the gate after it closes, it is usually too late to board, even if you can see the plane still parked. The airline cannot reopen the door without causing a serious delay and redoing final checks. So it is important to reach the gate on time.

Delays and Irregular Operations

If there is a weather delay or a mechanical problem, the gate agent might announce a new departure time. Passengers might have to wait in the gate area. Sometimes, if a delay is long, the airline provides meal or hotel vouchers, though rules vary. Gate agents must keep track of updates from maintenance or operations teams and let passengers know. They might also rebook passengers who can no longer make their connections.

In cases of major disruptions—like a big snowstorm—many flights might be canceled, and gates become crowded with travelers looking for solutions. Gate agents do their best to handle rebookings, but it can be very stressful for them and for passengers. Some travelers might seek help at an airline lounge or a customer service desk if the lines at the gate are too long.

International Gates and Border Controls

For international flights, gates can have extra steps. Passengers might need to show a passport or visa to the airline staff, so the agent confirms you can legally enter the destination country. Some airports have a separate secure zone for international departures, where you pass through additional checks before reaching the gate. The airline might also distribute immigration forms for you to fill out on the plane.

Upon arrival from abroad, you typically go through passport control and customs, but that is after the flight. The gate stage for international travel mainly involves ensuring each passenger has the necessary documents before boarding. If you cannot provide a valid passport or visa, the airline can refuse boarding.

Gate Amenities and New Innovations

Some modern gate areas have extra features. You might find charging poles with USB ports, interactive screens for kids, or quiet zones for business travelers. Airports try to make the gate area more comfortable because passengers often wait there for a while. Certain airports also use automated boarding gates. In this case, you scan your pass at a turnstile, which swings open if the system recognizes your booking. An agent still oversees the process, but it can speed things up.

Biometric technology is becoming more common. Some gates have face scanners that match your face with a passport photo on file. If the match is correct, the gate opens automatically. While this can be convenient, it raises questions about privacy and data storage. Airlines and governments follow rules about how they store and use biometric data, but the specifics differ by location.

How to Prepare for Smooth Boarding

Although we do not want to repeat earlier advice in detail, here are some points specifically about the gate experience:

- **Arrive Early:** Once you know your gate number, go there and wait. Gates can change or boarding might start early.
- **Listen for Announcements:** Keep your ears open for boarding group calls or seat changes.
- **Keep ID and Boarding Pass Ready:** Have them handy so you are not searching your bag last minute.
- **Ask Questions if Unsure:** Gate agents can clarify seat assignments, leftover overhead space, and connecting flight details.
- **Stay Nearby During Delays:** The gate agent might call you if an earlier flight opens up or if the airline changes the plan.

These small efforts can ensure you board smoothly and do not hold up the process.

Bringing It All Together

The gate is a final checkpoint in your trip through the airport. It is where the airline confirms who is truly getting on the plane and makes last-minute adjustments. Behind the scenes, the gate agent coordinates with the pilot, flight attendants, and ramp workers. The gate can be calm or hectic, depending on flight conditions, delays, or overbooking.

For passengers, the gate area is often a place of anticipation—everyone is ready to step aboard and begin the flight. Announcements keep you informed about the boarding order, upgrades, and any changes. Once your boarding pass is scanned and you walk down the jet bridge, you officially move from the busy airport environment to the airplane cabin, where your next focus is finding your seat and preparing for departure.

Although the gate might seem like just another waiting spot in the airport, it is one of the most essential links in air travel. Every step—scanning boarding passes, checking passports, assisting special needs passengers, and managing overhead bin space—helps to ensure a safe, well-organized flight. By understanding what happens here, you will feel more confident and prepared the next time you walk up to the gate agent and step onto the plane.

CHAPTER 9: THE PEOPLE WHO WORK AT AIRPORTS

Airports are busy places with many activities happening at once. Planes land and take off, travelers move in and out of terminals, and bags get sorted behind the scenes. None of this can happen without the people who work at airports. They have different jobs but share one goal: to keep everything running in a smooth and safe way. This chapter will explore the many roles you can find at an airport, from those who help passengers face to face to those who stay behind the scenes keeping systems in good shape.

Introduction to Airport Workers

Walk into any major airport, and you will see people in uniforms, people behind counters, and people driving small vehicles on the ramp. Others might be in offices or around the runways. All of these workers make up the airport team. Some are employed by the airport itself, and some work for airlines, security companies, or government agencies. A few work for private businesses that rent space inside the airport. Despite their different employers, they often communicate and cooperate. A large airport might feel like a city, and these workers are its citizens.

It helps to remember that each group has its own tasks. Some staff focus on customer service, making sure travelers get where they need to go. Others concentrate on safety, watching for anything unusual. Another group handles technical tasks, like repairing equipment or cleaning runways. In short, many roles come together so flights can operate on time and people can have a positive experience.

Airline Customer Service Staff

When you first arrive at the airport to check in, you likely meet airline customer service staff. These are the people at the ticket counters and bag drop desks who help you get your boarding pass and hand over your checked bags. They answer questions about flight times, seat assignments, or baggage weight limits. If you have a connecting flight, they can confirm whether your luggage will go all the way to your final stop. They also handle ticket changes if something in your travel plan needs adjusting.

Customer service staff work under pressure, especially at busy times or when flights get delayed. They must stay calm, offer solutions, and keep lines moving. Their training includes learning the airline's computer systems to look up passenger records, switch seats, or issue refunds. They also follow specific rules on baggage. Sometimes, they need to explain extra fees or items that are not allowed on the plane. Their goal is to keep travelers informed and comfortable before they head to security.

Gate Agents

A little deeper into the terminal, you will meet gate agents. These staff members manage the final steps before you get on the plane. They check boarding passes, announce boarding groups, and assist travelers who need special help. Gate agents also handle seat upgrades if the airline allows them, or place people on standby if the flight is full. If a flight is overbooked, the gate agents might ask if anyone is willing to take a later flight in exchange for a voucher. They have to keep track of who boards the plane, make sure each passenger scans their pass, and sort out any last-minute seat swaps.

Gate agents need strong communication skills and quick thinking. If there is a delay, they must explain the reason to waiting passengers. If they notice a traveler missing when it is almost time to close the flight, they announce a final call. When the plane is ready, they pass final numbers—like how many people are on board—to the flight deck crew. They also coordinate with ramp teams to confirm how many bags got loaded. Then, after everyone boards, they shut the door and officially release the flight for pushback.

Flight Attendants (Briefly at the Airport)

While flight attendants spend most of their time on the airplane, they begin and end their work at the airport. They arrive early to gather in a crew room, meet the pilots, and review flight details. Sometimes, they walk through the terminal in uniform, greeting passengers or answering quick questions. Though they do not stay in the terminal as long as gate agents, they are part of the airport scene. If you see them near the gate, it may be because they are switching flights or waiting for their next plane. Flight attendants focus on passenger comfort and safety once you board, but they also perform duties on the ground, like ensuring onboard supplies are ready.

Airport Security Officers

Security officers are dedicated to keeping everyone safe by checking bags and scanning travelers for dangerous items. You meet them at the security checkpoint, where they inspect carry-on luggage using x-ray machines and sometimes perform pat-downs or more detailed checks. Although we have looked at the security process before, it is good to note that these officers are trained professionals who stay watchful for anything suspicious. They also patrol around the terminal, hallways, and sometimes the perimeter fences, making sure no one is in a restricted area without authorization.

Security officers must follow strict guidelines. They learn how to spot threats on an x-ray screen, how to handle tricky situations, and how to remain polite even if a passenger is upset. They also conduct random checks on baggage. In the event of an emergency or evacuation, they help direct people to safety. Some airports have both private security officers and government agents. Together, these teams protect the airport from dangerous objects or activities.

Immigration and Customs Officers

For international airports, you can find immigration officers who check passports when travelers arrive from other countries. They verify if each passenger is allowed to enter the country by looking at visas or other documents. They might ask questions, like how long you plan to stay or where you will stay. Customs officers, on the other hand, inspect items people bring in, making sure no forbidden goods enter the country. They watch for banned foods, plants, or items that require special taxes or permits.

These officers have a big responsibility. They control the country's borders and keep track of what moves in and out. They often work in an area separate from the main domestic terminal. When flights land, travelers from abroad follow signs to the immigration and customs area. The officers there might use special databases to confirm if a passport is valid or flagged. Though some travelers find these checks stressful, they are essential for national security and controlling contraband.

Airport Management and Administration

Airports themselves have management teams that plan how the entire facility operates. This includes an airport director or manager, plus various departments like finance, marketing, operations, and human resources. They oversee budgets, building projects, and relationships with airlines. If an airline wants to add new flights, they often work with airport management to find suitable times and gates.

Administration staff also handle daily tasks like paying bills and arranging staff schedules. If the airport wants to improve the runway or expand a terminal, the management team partners with architects and construction crews. They also keep up with regulations from national and international agencies that govern flight safety. Without strong leadership, the airport could not grow or adapt to changes in aviation.

Maintenance and Facilities Teams

Airports are full of machinery. Escalators, moving walkways, air conditioning units, runway lights, and even the baggage belts all need upkeep. Maintenance workers specialize in fixing and inspecting these systems. If a conveyor belt stops working, they must respond quickly so luggage does not pile up. If the runway lights fail, they must repair them before night or poor weather sets in.

Some maintenance staff focus on electrical systems, while others do plumbing, carpentry, or mechanical repairs. Their jobs can be challenging because airports rarely shut down. They often do repairs at night or during off-peak hours to reduce disruptions. They also check the condition of runways and taxiways, patching cracks or repainting markings if needed. In winter, teams might handle de-icing of walkways or clearing snow around terminals.

Runway and Airfield Operations Staff

Aside from the main terminal, the airfield has specialists who keep the runways and taxiways safe. These crews inspect the pavement, remove debris, and help with wildlife control. Birds near runways can be a hazard. Some staff use special vehicles or sounds to scare birds away, reducing the chance of a bird strike. If a plane leaves bits of tire rubber on the runway, the team may clean it up so it does not become a hazard.

Airfield staff also manage lighting systems that guide pilots during takeoff and landing, especially at night or in fog. They may drive around to test if each light works. In big airports, they sometimes coordinate closure of one runway for maintenance, redirecting landings to another. This job requires attention to detail because a small problem on the runway can cause big safety issues.

Firefighters and Rescue Services

Every commercial airport has its own firefighting department ready for emergencies. These firefighters have special training to handle aircraft fires, fuel spills, and other unique problems that can happen around planes. Their trucks can spray water or foam to douse burning fuel. They also carry rescue equipment to help passengers exit a plane if it has a rough landing. Airport firefighters are often on standby near the runways, able to respond quickly if an inbound flight reports trouble.

They do regular drills to practice emergency landings or accidents. Sometimes, they train together with local city fire departments to coordinate efforts. The goal is to be prepared for unlikely but serious events. In day-to-day operations, these teams might also handle smaller incidents, such as a kitchen fire in an airport restaurant or a person needing first aid. They form a crucial line of defense for overall airport safety.

Airport Police

Airports often have their own police force or a dedicated branch of local law enforcement on site. These officers look out for criminal behavior, assist with traffic control around passenger drop-off areas, and help with lost or stolen property reports. They also manage any serious security threats, such as suspicious bags or people causing danger. Airport police know the layout of the terminals, making them able to respond fast to any alarm or alert.

They might also be involved in checking that restricted areas remain secure. Sometimes, they work with intelligence agencies if they suspect a traveler has illegal intentions. Police officers may set up random checks or walk around with trained dogs that can sniff out drugs or explosives. Just by being present, they help discourage crime and keep the atmosphere calm.

Medical and First Aid Personnel

In large airports, thousands of people pass through each day, so medical issues can arise. Some travelers feel unwell after a long flight, or they might trip and get injured. That is why many airports have a clinic or a first aid station staffed by medical workers or paramedics. They treat minor problems or arrange an ambulance if someone needs to go to the hospital. The medical team also knows how to handle emergencies like heart attacks, where quick action can save lives.

In many countries, airports are required to have defibrillators available in case someone has a cardiac event. Staff might get basic training on how to use them. The presence of medical professionals helps ensure that travelers can get help right away if they become sick while flying or waiting for a connecting flight.

Retail and Food Service Staff

Beyond the operational side, airports have numerous shops and restaurants. Staff at these places might be employed by brand-name stores or local businesses that rent space. Their job is to sell products, serve meals, and provide a bit of comfort to travelers. Whether it is a coffee shop, a gift store, or a bookstore, these workers greet customers, handle sales, and keep shelves stocked. The environment can be fast-paced, especially when flights arrive at peak times.

Restaurant and cafe workers might specialize in quick service, so travelers can eat before they board. Others focus on sit-down meals for those with longer waits. Some airports have staff who deliver food to gates or operate vending machines around the terminal. All these roles give passengers more options, making the airport less stressful if they have time before the flight.

Cleaning and Sanitation Teams

Keeping an airport clean is no small task. Cleaning crews work around the clock to vacuum floors, wipe seats, and empty trash cans. They also sanitize restrooms, clean up spills, and make sure high-touch areas, such as handrails and elevator buttons, are disinfected. When thousands of people walk through every day, dirt and trash can build up quickly, so these teams have a strict schedule to follow.

In the terminal, you might see cleaning staff pushing carts with supplies, quietly working in the background. On the airfield side, other crews handle bigger tasks, like clearing dirt off runways or cleaning windows in the control tower. During times of heightened health concerns, the airport might add extra disinfecting measures, and these crews become even more important for public safety.

Snow Removal and Weather-Related Workers

In places with cold climates, winter can bring heavy snow and ice that might cause flight delays. Airports have workers trained to remove snow from runways, taxiways, and parking areas. They drive large plows and snow blowers to clear the airfield. They also spread de-icing chemicals on the pavement to prevent ice buildup. Sometimes, they must act quickly if a sudden snowstorm hits, so the airport can stay operational.

Apart from snow, strong winds or flooding can also cause problems. Certain staff monitor weather reports closely, deciding whether to close a runway or delay flights for safety. If a storm is expected, they position equipment and staff in advance to handle it. These roles require good teamwork, because even a short period of runway closure affects many flights.

Engineers and Planners

Larger airports might have a dedicated engineering department. These experts handle construction, remodeling, and expansion plans. They decide how to add gates or build new sections of the terminal. They also advise on materials that can handle heavy airplane traffic. Sometimes, they design systems that help move passengers quickly, like automated trains between terminals.

Planners look at projected passenger numbers to see if the airport will need more gates or bigger waiting areas in the future. They also consider environmental rules, local community concerns, and cost. Engineers work with architects to plan new buildings or upgrade existing ones. Once construction begins, they oversee the process to ensure everything meets regulations.

Information Desk and Passenger Assistance Staff

Many airports have information desks or roaming staff whose main job is to help travelers find their way. They give directions to gates, restrooms, and lounges.

They might speak multiple languages to assist international visitors. If someone gets lost, these staff members check maps or flight schedules to guide them. They can also suggest the quickest route if your connection time is short.

At times, you will see staff with signs offering help to older people, families, or anyone who seems confused. They often deal with questions about local transportation options, hotels, or tourist spots. This makes the airport more welcoming. Some volunteers might help direct crowds on busy days or assist in special events. Although they might not wear an airline uniform, their role is crucial for smooth passenger flow.

Animal and Pet Handling Staff

Airports that permit pets or service animals might have staff or specialized contractors who handle animal care. If someone is sending a pet as cargo, these employees ensure the crate is secure and that the pet has water. For service animals traveling in the cabin, staff might check that the right documents are in place. Large airports can have designated animal relief areas with artificial turf and cleaning supplies.

Some employees focus on wildlife hazards around the airfield. They keep geese, deer, or other animals away from runways. They might use fences, noisemakers, or safe capture methods to relocate animals. By doing so, they reduce the danger of collisions between planes and wildlife. While not the most visible role, it is an essential one for flight safety.

Coordination and Teamwork Among Airport Workers

An airport runs smoothly only if these different groups stay in touch. Gate agents must coordinate with ramp staff so that passengers' bags load onto the correct plane. Security officers might notify airline managers if there is an unusual situation, so flights can be delayed until it is resolved. If the runway needs repair, maintenance leaders tell air traffic controllers to reroute planes.

Airport leaders organize daily or weekly meetings to discuss upcoming busy seasons, special flights, or planned construction. They might also have direct communication lines in case of emergencies. A strong sense of teamwork helps them solve problems fast. For example, if a flight must land urgently, multiple teams—fire, medical, ground operations—jump into action at once. Everyone knows their role, preventing confusion.

Why These Roles Matter

Every person who works at an airport contributes to the overall success of air travel. If security officers are not thorough, safety is at risk. If gate agents are not organized, flights could leave late. If maintenance teams do not fix escalators or runway lights, travelers might face big delays. Even the smaller tasks—like cleaning windows or emptying trash bins—improve the experience for passengers.

Airports are gateways for business, vacation, and family visits. They help connect distant cities and support economic growth. Without the people who manage the daily tasks, planes would have nowhere to park, travelers would not know where to go, and important cargo would not reach its destination. By appreciating each airport job, you see how all these moving parts fit together.

CHAPTER 10: THE GROUND CREW AND VEHICLES

Look outside the window while waiting in an airport terminal, and you will spot all sorts of vehicles zipping around the airplane. Some carry luggage, some transport fuel, and others move passengers to smaller planes parked farther away. These vehicles, along with the people who drive them, are known as the ground crew and ground support. They form the backbone of airport operations on the ramp (the area around planes). This chapter focuses on who they are, what they do, and the specialized vehicles they use.

The Role of the Ground Crew

Before an airplane can take off, it needs many preparations. That is where the ground crew comes in. Their duties include loading bags, refueling, pushing back the plane from the gate, and even de-icing during cold weather. They also guide the pilot when parking the plane, using bright wands or hand signals to direct the aircraft's nose to the right spot. In short, ground crew tasks happen between flights to make sure each plane is ready for departure on time.

Members of the ground crew often wear reflective vests so they can be seen among moving vehicles and planes. They must follow strict safety rules because they work close to aircraft engines and heavy machinery. Good communication is essential. Ramp workers use radios or hand signals to coordinate with each other and with the cockpit. If a single bag is missed or a cart drives into the wrong area, flights could be delayed or accidents could happen.

Baggage Tractors and Carts

Among the most common vehicles on the ramp are baggage tractors (sometimes called tugs). These small but powerful trucks tow one or more baggage carts linked like a short train. Inside each cart, suitcases and cargo boxes are stacked. These vehicles shuttle luggage from the baggage sorting area to the plane and back again. When you see a tractor pulling several carts, it might be delivering outgoing bags or picking up arriving ones.

Baggage tractors must be easy to maneuver around tight gates and under aircraft wings. They are designed to handle extra weight and climb ramps leading into cargo handling areas. Drivers are trained to park the carts close to the aircraft's cargo doors so baggage handlers can load or unload quickly. On rainy or snowy days, the carts often have covers or tarps to protect luggage from the elements.

Pushback Tractors

When it is time for a plane to leave the gate, it usually cannot drive backward on its own. Instead, ground staff use a pushback tractor (also called a tug) to move the airplane away from the gate in reverse. Pushback tractors have large, sturdy tires and a low profile to fit under the nose of the aircraft. Some connect to the plane's nose gear using a tow bar, while others are towbarless and clamp onto the nose wheels.

Operating a pushback tractor requires skill. The driver must coordinate with the pilot, who releases the parking brake and follows ground instructions. The pilot might turn on some power so the aircraft systems can run, but the engines may remain at idle or off for safety. The pushback driver uses radio communication to confirm each step. Once the plane is positioned correctly on the taxiway, the driver detaches and signals the cockpit. The aircraft can then start taxiing forward under its own power.

Belt Loaders

Getting suitcases into the cargo hold of a plane can be tricky if the door is high above the ground. That is why belt loaders are used. They look like small trucks with a moving conveyor belt on top. The belt can be raised or lowered to align with the cargo door. Ground crew place bags on the belt one by one, and a coworker inside the plane stacks them. This process helps speed up loading and reduces the strain of lifting heavy items by hand.

Belt loaders have to be parked carefully. If they bump into the aircraft's body or door, they can cause damage. Drivers watch their mirrors and sometimes rely on a spotter to guide them. The belt itself can be turned on or off and might move in different directions. Some belt loaders can also fold at an angle for smaller planes. The key is to position it so there is little chance of dropping suitcases or hitting the plane.

Cargo Loaders for Large Aircraft

For big airplanes, like wide-body jets that fly long distances, there are containerized cargo holds. These planes store luggage and freight in metal or sturdy containers. Large cargo loader vehicles lift these containers to the proper height and slide them onto rails inside the plane's hold. These loaders often have platforms that can raise or lower, plus a mechanism to move containers in and out. The driver lines up the loader with the plane's door, then operates the platform using a control panel.

Cargo loaders can handle heavy loads, sometimes thousands of pounds in a single container. Their wheels and hydraulic systems are built for stability because a sudden drop could damage the goods or injure workers. Once the container is inside, cargo staff secure it in place. The process is reversed when the plane lands, so the containers can be offloaded onto waiting trucks or the airport's cargo facility.

Fuel Trucks and Hydrant Systems

Airplanes need a lot of fuel for each flight. Fuel trucks are common sights on the ramp, equipped with large tanks and hoses. They drive to the aircraft's wing or belly fueling point, connect a hose, and fill the plane's tanks with the correct type of aviation fuel. The driver monitors gauges and checks with the pilot or a dispatcher about how much fuel is needed. Sometimes, more than one fuel truck is used if the plane is very large or the flight is very long.

At some airports, there is a hydrant system beneath the tarmac, similar to pipes carrying water, but in this case, they carry jet fuel. In those airports, a smaller vehicle called a hydrant cart connects the plane to the underground fuel supply. This can speed up the process, because the aircraft can be fueled without a big truck. Still, careful checks are done to prevent leaks, spills, or fire hazards. The ground crew checks the fuel's quality and also ensures they do not exceed the plane's weight limits.

Catering Trucks

When you eat or drink on a plane, most items come from airport catering services. Catering trucks are tall vehicles with a box on top that can be raised up to the airplane's door, often near the front galley. Workers load and unload food carts, beverage supplies, and other items like napkins or trash bags. They must also keep track of special meals, such as those for travelers with dietary needs.

These trucks often have refrigeration units to keep food fresh, along with heating elements to keep hot meals warm. Because they get so close to the plane, the driver must align the truck body precisely to the door. Flight attendants or catering staff might be inside, ready to move the carts into the galley. Timing is important because the plane's turnaround schedule can be tight. If catering runs late, the flight might depart behind schedule.

Lavatory Service Trucks

Planes have onboard restrooms that need to be emptied and refilled with fresh water. Lavatory service trucks do this job. They attach a hose to the plane's waste tank, drain it into the truck's holding tank, and then flush the system with cleaning fluids. They also refill the plane's water supply for the sinks and toilets. This is not the most glamorous task, but it is crucial for hygiene and passenger comfort.

These trucks must connect hoses carefully to avoid leaks or unpleasant odors on the ramp. Workers wear protective gear, like gloves and face covers, as a safeguard. Once the job is done, the waste is transported to a proper disposal facility. If an airline forgets or skips this step, passengers on the next flight might find the restrooms out of service, so lavatory trucks are an essential part of the turnaround process.

Water Service Vehicles

Some aircraft also need extra drinkable water stored in a separate tank for making coffee or tea onboard. Water service trucks carry clean, potable water that can be pumped into the plane's holding tank. This is different from the water used in restrooms, which might not be considered drinkable. Water service trucks have pumps, gauges, and hoses to ensure the water is safe. Crews check sanitation before filling the plane's tank, because it is important for passenger health.

Passenger Buses

At some airports, especially where planes park far from the terminal or if there are not enough gates with jet bridges, passengers ride buses from the gate to the plane. These airport buses are designed to hold large groups of people and have wide doors for easy entry. They may travel on a set path around the ramp, stopping at the aircraft stairs. After everyone boards or deplanes, the bus returns for more passengers. The driver must stay aware of ramp rules and watch out for other vehicles or planes moving nearby.

In certain parts of the world, using a bus to board is common because it allows the airport to handle more flights than they have gates. It can also be more flexible if an airline decides to park a plane in a remote spot for a short time. Passengers might get a closer view of the airfield this way, but they must follow crew instructions for safety.

De-Icing Vehicles

In cold climates, ice or snow can build up on an airplane's wings, which is dangerous for flight. De-icing vehicles solve this by spraying a heated fluid (often a mixture of glycol and water) onto the plane's surfaces. The fluid melts or prevents ice. These vehicles have a raised platform or a boom arm that can spray the top of the wings, tail, and other areas the pilot requests.

De-icing crews wear protective clothing and communicate by radio with the cockpit. The pilot might say, "We need Type I fluid on the wings," or ask for a different type that lasts longer to prevent ice buildup while waiting for takeoff. Once the plane is de-iced, it must take off within a certain time window before ice can reform. De-icing is a precise operation that requires knowledge of weather conditions and fluid properties. If done incorrectly or not at all, the aircraft might lose lift or experience other hazards during takeoff.

Follow-Me Cars

When airplanes land or need to move in complex areas, a "follow-me" car sometimes guides them. These are small vehicles with bright markings, lights on top, and the words "Follow Me" on the back. The follow-me car drives ahead of the plane along the correct taxiways or to the correct parking spot, especially if the pilot is not familiar with that airport's layout. This is more common at smaller airports or in conditions of low visibility.

The driver of the follow-me car communicates with air traffic control to confirm the route. They must keep a safe distance ahead, so the pilot has time to turn or stop if needed. The pilot watches the car's signals and follows it closely. Once the plane is near the gate or runway, the follow-me car peels away so the pilot can finish parking or line up for takeoff. It is a helpful way to prevent confusion on the ground.

Aircraft Rescue and Firefighting Vehicles

We learned in a previous chapter about airport firefighters. Their vehicles are designed to respond quickly to any emergency involving an airplane. These fire trucks often have large foam cannons on top, special tires for rough terrain, and huge water or foam tanks. Some can drive at high speeds across grass or dirt areas near runways. They also carry rescue tools to cut through an airplane's fuselage if a door is blocked.

Aircraft rescue and firefighting vehicles usually park in a dedicated fire station near the runway for fast response times. If an incoming flight reports a problem—like hot brakes, engine trouble, or a landing gear issue—firefighters stand by with engines running, ready to spray foam or water if needed. These vehicles train with practice drills, often using old planes or mockups to simulate real incidents.

Maintenance and Service Vans

Besides the bigger trucks, you will see smaller vans or pickup trucks moving around. Maintenance teams use these to fix broken lights or signs on the ramp. Sometimes, they carry replacement parts, tools, and safety cones. If a plane's gate has a broken jet bridge or an electrical fault, a service van arrives with a small crew to do repairs. These vans might also deliver spare tires for baggage carts or re-stock safety gear around the apron.

Many maintenance vans have bright flashing beacons on top so pilots and other drivers see them clearly. Airport rules require them to move carefully, especially near taxiways. Drivers often need clearance from ground control before crossing those paths. In busy airports, every crossing must be timed to avoid an oncoming plane.

Ramp Safety and Hazards

With so many vehicles in one place, ramp safety is critical. Ground crews must watch for moving propellers or jet engines that can create strong blasts of air. They also need to avoid collisions with other vehicles. Markings on the ground help define safe zones, traffic lanes, and parking spots. Drivers follow speed limits and yield rules. If someone misses a sign, they could end up where they should not be.

Another hazard is the noise level. Airplane engines are extremely loud. That is why ground staff wear earmuffs or earplugs. Some tasks require wearing goggles or hard hats if there is a risk of falling objects. Airports have strict safety checks, and staff receive training on how to use reflective gear, watch out for fueling lines, and handle slippery conditions in rain or snow.

Communication Methods

Ground crews communicate in a few ways:

- **Hand Signals:** When guiding a plane in or out, some ground staff use orange wands or batons. Specific motions tell the pilot to slow, turn, or stop.
- **Headsets and Radios:** Many tasks, like refueling or pushback, involve radio contact with the cockpit. A headset allows the ground worker to speak to the flight deck, confirming steps like "Parking brake off" or "We are clear from the aircraft."
- **Company Radios and Apps:** Staff may use a private radio channel or mobile apps to coordinate baggage transfers, get updates on flight schedules, and request extra vehicles.

Clear communication avoids mistakes. If a pilot misunderstands a hand signal, they could steer the plane into ground equipment. If a fueling truck loses contact, it might overfill a tank. So, the entire ground crew aims for accurate messaging at each step.

Training and Certification

Working in ground operations is not something anyone can do without training. Staff must learn how to operate specialized vehicles, follow safety protocols, and carry out each task correctly. Many airports require a driver's permit for ramp vehicles, separate from a normal driver's license. Workers may also take lessons in hazardous materials handling, since some cargo can be flammable or delicate.

Refueling staff must understand the types of fuel, how to check for contaminants, and how to ground the plane and truck to avoid sparks. De-icing crews study the types of fluid, concentration levels, and how weather affects ice. Everyone receives recurring training, because airport procedures and technology keep changing. Some staff specialize in certain vehicles; others rotate through multiple tasks.

Environmental Considerations

Airports focus on cutting down emissions and pollution. Vehicles on the ramp often use diesel or gas, but some airports switch to electric baggage tractors and greener fuels. This reduces fumes and noise. Airports might also set rules about idling—drivers should turn off engines if they are parked for more than a few minutes.

De-icing fluids, if not handled properly, can pollute nearby water sources. Modern airports have drainage systems and water treatment plans to capture used de-icing fluid and prevent it from entering rivers. Fuel trucks also have strict guidelines for spill response. In a spill, ground crews place absorbent materials around the area and clean up quickly to protect the environment and prevent fires.

Daily Challenges for Ground Crews

Ground operations are high-pressure because flights run on tight schedules. If a bag cart is late or a pushback tractor breaks, the flight might depart behind schedule. Weather adds more complications. Heavy rain makes surfaces slippery, while lightning can force ramp workers to stay indoors until it passes, halting fueling or baggage loading. In snowy conditions, they must remove ice from the plane and keep the tarmac clear.

They also handle unexpected events. A bag can tear open, scattering items on the pavement. An engine might need a quick fix. Ground crews have to remain flexible, adapting to each situation while keeping safety first. They often work in shifts, covering early mornings, late nights, weekends, and holidays. The ramp never really closes at busy airports, so there is always a team on duty.

How Ground Crew and Vehicles Fit into the Big Picture

Every successful flight depends on ground crew and their vehicles. From fueling to loading bags, from guiding planes to de-icing in winter, these tasks must happen quickly and carefully. Even the best pilots and cabin crews rely on ground teams to give them a safe, well-prepared airplane. Passengers might not see each detail—such as the pushback procedure or the fueling checks—but these behind-the-scenes activities keep things running.

The variety of specialized vehicles you see outside the terminal highlights the complexity of air travel. Each machine has a purpose, whether it is a belt loader for suitcases or a firefighter truck ready for emergencies. These vehicles are operated by trained workers who brave weather, tight deadlines, and noisy conditions to send planes off on time. Together, they form a network of support that covers every aspect of ground handling.

CHAPTER 11: REPAIRS AND MAINTENANCE

Airports are large sites with many structures and systems that must stay in good condition. This includes runways, taxiways, terminals, lights, and ground vehicles. If something breaks or starts to wear out, it can create problems for flights and for people visiting the airport. That is why repairs and maintenance are so important. In this chapter, we will look at how airports keep their buildings, runways, and other facilities working well, why maintenance matters for safety, and what happens when major repairs are needed.

What Maintenance Means at an Airport

Maintenance at an airport is not just about fixing broken parts. It also includes regular checks to make sure everything is safe and reliable. For instance, workers might look at the runway surface, the terminals, the baggage equipment, and all the lights and signs that help planes move. If they find a small crack in the pavement, they repair it before it becomes a bigger problem. When a light bulb in a runway edge light burns out, they replace it quickly so pilots can see where to land at night.

This careful attention is crucial because airports operate nearly all day, every day. Unlike some buildings that can close for a while to fix things, an airport is often running around the clock. Maintenance teams plan their work so it disrupts flights as little as possible. Sometimes they might do bigger jobs late at night or during periods when fewer planes are scheduled to land or take off.

The Teams That Handle Maintenance

You might wonder who takes care of all these tasks. Different teams focus on different areas:

1. **Runway and Airfield Maintenance Crew**
    - This group keeps the runways, taxiways, and parking ramps in good shape. They check for cracks, potholes, or signs of damage. They also maintain the painted markings, such as centerlines and runway numbers.
2. **Building Maintenance**
    - Another team looks after the terminal itself: floors, windows, escalators, elevators, and air conditioning systems. They might fix a leaky pipe in a restroom or replace ceiling tiles that got damp.
3. **Electrical and Lighting Specialists**
    - Because airports have many lights—on runways, taxiways, ramps, and terminals—there are specialists who know how to repair and replace bulbs, wiring, and circuits. These experts also care for backup generators that keep the airport lit if the main power goes out.
4. **Vehicle and Equipment Mechanics**
    - The airport owns many vehicles, like baggage tractors, fire trucks, snowplows, and security cars. Mechanics keep these running by changing oil, replacing parts, and checking the engines. They also maintain equipment such as belt loaders and pushback tractors.
5. **IT and Electronics Crew**
    - Modern airports depend on computers for flight schedules, security systems, and baggage handling. If a server or network cable fails, these experts fix it. They might also maintain the screens that show arrival and departure times.

These teams work together, sometimes coordinating with airline staff and air traffic control. They follow a schedule of inspections to catch issues early. If a problem is urgent—like a broken escalator causing passenger traffic jams—they fix it right away.

Taking Care of the Runways

Runways are among the most critical parts of an airport. They allow planes to take off and land safely, but they also face heavy use. Airplane tires can leave rubber marks, and the surface must handle the enormous weight of aircraft day after day. Over time, temperature changes, rain, or snow can wear down the surface, creating cracks or uneven spots. Maintenance crews fix these quickly because a damaged runway can become dangerous.

One common method is to fill cracks with special sealants to keep water out. If water seeps into a crack and then freezes, it can cause bigger splits in the concrete or asphalt. Sometimes, workers must remove a portion of the runway surface and pave it again. They plan these projects for periods when the runway can be closed temporarily, so they do not disrupt flights too much. In busy airports, they might do partial closures—closing one runway while keeping others open. At smaller airports with just one runway, they have to schedule repairs for times with fewer flights, or else flights will need to be moved to another airport.

Besides the surface, there are edge lights, approach lights, and signs that mark taxiways and runways. Each of these can burn out or become damaged. Maintenance teams have a checklist to test them regularly, sometimes driving along runways at night to see which lights need replacing. They also keep spare parts on hand so they do not lose time searching for them when a bulb burns out.

Pavement Management Programs

Many airports use a "pavement management program," a system that monitors how runways and taxiways age over time. Inspectors might walk or drive across the airfield, noting cracks, ruts, or areas that look worn. They record these in a computer system that assigns a rating to each stretch of pavement. This helps the airport decide when to do minor fixes versus major resurfacing.

Major resurfacing is a big job. It might involve scraping away the old surface and laying down new asphalt or concrete. Workers need large machines—like pavers, rollers, and milling machines—to do the work quickly but thoroughly. After the new surface goes down, they repaint the runway numbers, centerlines, and touchdown markers. Then they test friction, ensuring airplane tires can grip the runway well, especially in rainy conditions.

Keeping Terminals in Top Condition

The terminal is where passengers spend the most time. To remain welcoming, it must be clean, comfortable, and functional. That means the floors, walls, and ceilings should be free from cracks or leaks. The escalators, elevators, and walkways should run smoothly. The air conditioning and heating systems must keep temperatures pleasant. And restrooms must be stocked and working properly.

If something breaks, like an escalator, maintenance workers may put up signs directing people to stairs or another escalator, then fix the broken parts. Sometimes they can do these fixes fast, but bigger repairs might take a while, requiring special parts from the manufacturer. Modern terminals also have many glass walls so that travelers can watch planes. This glass needs cleaning to remove smudges or dirt. When glass panels break, a team replaces them carefully, often at night or during quieter times.

Heating, Ventilation, and Air Conditioning (HVAC)

Inside the terminal, the HVAC system is crucial for passenger comfort. A big airport might have miles of air ducts, multiple chiller units for cold air, and boilers for heat. Maintenance staff check air filters, thermostats, and sensors to be sure everything works. If a chiller breaks during a hot day, the terminal might become uncomfortably warm, so a quick response is needed. Regular inspections help spot worn parts or leaks in the system before they cause problems. With thousands of people passing through, good ventilation also helps keep the air fresh and reduce the spread of germs.

Electrical Systems and Emergency Power

The airport's electrical system must be very reliable. If the lights go out, flights cannot safely operate, and passengers would be stuck in the dark. Hence, airports have backup generators or battery systems to keep essential services running if the main power fails. Maintenance crews test these backups frequently. They also check transformers, circuit breakers, and wiring throughout the terminal and airfield.

Runway and taxiway lights have special cables buried underground. If a cable is damaged by water or a rodent, the light might not work. Workers locate the problem using instruments that detect breaks in the line. They might need to dig up a section of the ground to replace the cable. This kind of repair requires close coordination with air traffic control because they may need to close part of the taxiway or runway while the work is done.

Caring for Ground Vehicles and Equipment

From baggage tractors to snowplows, all airport vehicles need regular upkeep. Technicians change oil, check brakes, and replace worn tires. Some airports keep a small fleet of cars for staff who inspect runways or move around the perimeter to check fences. These also need routine checks to stay reliable. Fuel trucks and fire trucks require even more attention due to safety rules. Fire trucks carry foam or water tanks that must not leak. Fuel trucks must be free from any risk of sparks near the fuel hose.

For belt loaders or pushback tractors, mechanics look at hydraulic systems, belts, and engines to confirm everything is working as it should. If winter brings a lot of snow, snowplows, sweepers, and de-icing vehicles see heavy action and might need part replacements. Having well-maintained vehicles helps keep flight schedules on time, because a breakdown can delay loading or refueling.

Scheduling Maintenance Work

Airports never fully stop operating, so scheduling repairs is a challenge. Small fixes can be handled quickly at any time, but big projects require careful planning. Maintenance managers meet with airlines, air traffic control, and sometimes with city or government officials to figure out the best timing. For example, if the airport wants to repave part of a runway, they will choose a period of low traffic or divert some flights to a different runway.

Often, major works are done overnight or on weekends. Crews might close a runway at midnight, work for several hours, and then reopen it by dawn. This way, flights are less disrupted. It can be hard on the workers, who might have to do many night shifts, but it keeps the airport functioning. In very large airports, there might be multiple runways, so closing one for maintenance is less of a problem. However, they still plan it carefully, because even one closed runway can slow down the flow of landings and takeoffs.

Handling Emergencies and Sudden Repairs

Not all repairs can be planned. Sometimes an airplane may experience a mechanical failure on the runway, like a burst tire, leaving debris or rubber on the pavement. In that case, emergency maintenance teams rush out to remove the debris and check if the surface got damaged. The airport might close that runway briefly until it is safe again.

In other cases, severe weather could damage parts of the terminal roof or break windows. A power surge might knock out some lights. Maintenance and repair teams respond right away, blocking off dangerous areas and starting repairs. For bigger emergencies, such as flooding or a fire, many different airport groups join forces. The goal is to keep travelers safe and restore normal operations quickly.

Keeping Things Clean

While we often think of "maintenance" as fixing mechanical parts, cleaning is also a big part of caring for an airport. Workers clean floors, carpets, windows, and seats to create a good environment. They also clean up litter on runways and ramps. Even a small object left on the runway can become a hazard if a plane's tires run over it. Some airports use special vehicles to sweep the runway regularly, picking up rocks, bolts, or other debris.

In regions with winter snow, de-icing fluid and salt can build up on roads and vehicle surfaces. Maintenance teams wash vehicles to prevent rust or corrosion. They also check drains to be sure melted snow can flow away rather than flooding. In warm climates, dust or sand can accumulate, so sweeper vehicles might be used to clear taxiways. A clean airport is not just nice to look at; it also keeps planes from being damaged by stray debris.

Inspections and Regulations

Airports must follow many rules set by aviation authorities. These rules require regular inspections of the runway's condition, the lighting systems, firefighting equipment, and more. Inspectors might visit unannounced to confirm the airport is meeting standards. If something does not pass inspection, the airport could face penalties, or they might be told to fix it right away.

Additionally, many airports follow an internally developed maintenance schedule. They might have daily checks, weekly checks, monthly checks, and yearly checks. Daily checks could include walking around the runway edges to spot any cracks or foreign objects. Weekly checks might involve testing backup generators. Yearly checks could include reviewing entire systems, like the air conditioning in the terminal. By following these routines, airports avoid big problems and keep everything in good shape.

Upgrading Facilities

Maintenance is not just about repairs—it also involves upgrading equipment to improve efficiency. Airports might replace older lights with LED bulbs that last longer and use less energy. They might install modern escalators that run only when someone is nearby, saving electricity. Or they might put in advanced baggage scanning systems that speed up the sorting process. These upgrades can reduce future maintenance work because the equipment is more reliable or easier to fix.

Sometimes, upgrades are needed to keep up with newer airplane models. If airlines start using bigger planes, the airport might reinforce the runway and taxiways to handle heavier loads. They might also expand the gates or waiting areas to hold more passengers. These are big projects that often happen over months or even years. While these projects are going on, maintenance teams help coordinate construction crews, making sure day-to-day operations can continue.

The Challenge of Older Airports

Some airports were built many decades ago and have older terminals, runways, or hangars. Keeping these facilities up to modern standards can be challenging. The electrical wiring might be outdated, or the original building materials could need special care. Maintenance teams have to learn about old design methods, so they do not accidentally weaken the structure. They might also need hard-to-find replacement parts.

Over time, airports usually plan renovations or expansions. For example, they might build a new terminal wing to replace an old one, or close an outdated runway and build a new one in a better spot. But as long as the old areas remain in use, they must be maintained. This can be expensive, so airport managers balance the costs of constant repairs against the cost of building something new.

Technology in Airport Maintenance

Advances in technology make maintenance easier and more precise:

- **Sensors and Monitoring:** Some runways have sensors that detect temperature, moisture, or cracks. Alerts go to a control center if something needs attention.
- **Drones:** A few airports are testing drones to inspect roofs or hard-to-reach places. A drone can capture high-resolution images, helping workers see cracks or damage without climbing.
- **Computerized Maintenance Management Systems (CMMS):** These are software tools that track every piece of equipment, schedule repairs, and record when tasks are done. If a baggage belt needs an oil change every certain number of hours, the system notifies the team.
- **Augmented Reality (AR):** In the future, a mechanic might wear AR glasses that display a machine's repair manual or highlight parts that need servicing.

By using these technologies, airports can predict failures before they happen and fix things sooner. This saves money, reduces downtime, and keeps the airport safer and more efficient.

The Importance of Proper Training

No matter how good the tools are, the people doing maintenance need strong skills. Mechanics must know how to work on specialized vehicles, such as pushback tractors or fire trucks. Electricians must understand airport lighting systems, which can be very different from household wiring. Pavement experts need to know about runway materials, while HVAC technicians must handle enormous air systems.

Regular training is key. Airport maintenance staff might attend workshops, receive certifications, or learn directly from experienced coworkers. They also must stay updated on new rules or technologies. Sometimes, manufacturers of specialized equipment (like baggage scanners) provide training classes so the airport's workers can learn to maintain the machines correctly.

Reducing Environmental Impact

As airports maintain and repair their facilities, they also watch out for environmental concerns. Old equipment might use lots of energy or produce harmful emissions. By upgrading to efficient systems—such as LED lighting or electric ground vehicles—the airport can cut pollution. When they fix runways or expand terminals, they might protect local habitats, recycle building materials, or use methods that lower water usage. During routine checks, they watch for oil leaks or chemical spills. This focus on the environment helps airports be better neighbors to the communities around them.

Working with Airlines

Airlines rent space at the airport—gates, ticket counters, and sometimes maintenance hangars for planes. They rely on the airport to keep runways and taxiways in top shape. If the airport needs to close a runway for repairs, the airlines might need to change flight schedules. This takes coordination. The airport tries to schedule repairs at times that cause the fewest flight disruptions, and the airlines must plan around it.

Airlines might have their own ground maintenance staff for tasks like checking ground service vehicles or cleaning gate areas. In such cases, the airport and airline teams share information about any repairs that could affect the airline's operations. Good communication helps both sides avoid confusion and delays.

Challenges and Costs

Maintaining an airport is expensive. Materials like asphalt, concrete, and lighting fixtures cost a lot, and skilled labor can be hard to find. Airports earn revenue from landing fees, passenger facility charges, and other sources. But they have to spend large amounts on upkeep. If an airport delays maintenance to save money, problems can grow worse and cost more in the long run. A cracked runway that is not fixed promptly might require a full resurfacing if water gets under the pavement.

Weather is another challenge. Extreme cold can freeze pipes and cause runways to crack. Very hot weather can make asphalt soft. Storms can flood areas or knock out power lines. Maintenance staff must be ready for anything. Some airports in hurricane-prone regions strengthen buildings and store extra supplies so they can recover faster after a storm.

Wrapping It All Up

An airport's success hinges on strong maintenance. From the runway's surface to the lights on the terminal walls, everything must work correctly for flights to be safe and on time. Maintenance teams and repair crews handle this responsibility. They check, fix, and sometimes replace parts of the airport's infrastructure, often working late nights or early mornings to avoid disruptions. They also keep a close watch on new technology and regulations, making sure the airport stays up to date.

If you ever see workers on the runway at night or spot a mechanic fixing an escalator, you will know how vital their role is. Without them, problems would pile up. Planes might face rough landings on damaged runways, or travelers might get stuck with broken escalators or no air conditioning. Thanks to these dedicated teams, airports remain safe, comfortable places—well-lit, well-maintained, and ready for the next wave of flights.

CHAPTER 12: EATING AND SHOPPING AT THE AIRPORT

An airport is not just a place to catch flights. It is also full of shops and eateries, big and small, where people can spend time while waiting for their plane. Some airports have entire sections devoted to dining and retail, making them feel a bit like shopping malls. Food and shopping might sound like a small part of air travel, but they serve many purposes. People who are hungry can grab a meal, those who forgot an item at home can buy it, and others enjoy a quick treat before they board. This chapter explains how these dining and shopping areas are set up, why they matter, and how they fit into the airport's overall plan.

Why Airports Have Shops and Restaurants

One major reason is convenience. Travelers might spend hours waiting for a connecting flight or arrive early to pass through security. During this time, they may want to eat, buy souvenirs, or pick up things like headphones, snacks, or reading material. If you forgot your phone charger at home, you can often find a new one in an airport shop.

Another reason is revenue. Airports earn money by leasing space to restaurants, cafes, and retail stores. That helps them pay for the cost of running the airport, from cleaning terminals to maintaining runways. Many airports look for popular brands that will attract travelers. They may also include local or regional shops to give visitors a taste of the area's culture.

The Layout of Dining and Retail Areas

Most terminals have a mix of shops and eateries before and after the security checkpoint. You might see a coffee stand near the check-in area for people who have not gone through security yet. Once you clear security, there is usually a larger range of options. You might find restaurants with seating, small snack kiosks, souvenir stores, and duty-free shops (especially if you are flying internationally).

The layout often encourages people to walk by many stores on their way to the gates. Airport planners do this so travelers notice the shops and might stop in. If you have a few hours until boarding, you might wander around, find a place to eat, or pick up gifts for friends back home. Big airports sometimes call these areas "concourses" or "piers," with wide corridors lined by shops on both sides.

Types of Eateries

Airport dining options can range from quick takeout stands to fancy sit-down places. Below are some common types:

1. **Fast Food**
    - Well-known burger, pizza, or sandwich chains often appear in airports. They are quick and familiar, which suits travelers who want something fast.
2. **Coffee Shops and Cafés**
    - Many travelers want coffee or tea. Coffee shops also sell pastries, muffins, and sandwiches. Some people like to sit for a while, use Wi-Fi, or watch planes through the windows.
3. **Sit-Down Restaurants**
    - These serve full meals, such as steaks, pasta, or local specialties. They can be more expensive, but they give you a chance to relax if you have a long layover.
4. **Bars and Lounges**
    - Some travelers enjoy a soft drink or other beverage before their flight. Bars might also serve small snacks or finger foods. In some airports, these are near the gates so you can watch boarding announcements.
5. **Grab-and-Go Kiosks**
    - Perfect for short connections, these kiosks sell sandwiches, salads, bottled drinks, or packaged snacks. You can buy quickly and head to your gate.

Some airports try to include local cuisine as well. If you are in a region famous for seafood, you might find a seafood eatery. If it is known for certain pastries or desserts, there could be a bakery stall selling them. That way, visitors get a small taste of local flavor without leaving the airport.

Hygiene and Food Safety

Serving food to thousands of people every day requires strict cleanliness. Airport eateries follow health guidelines to ensure the food is safe. Kitchens and serving areas must be cleaned often, and staff members might wear gloves or hairnets. Health inspectors can visit any time to check if rules are followed. If something is not right—like a refrigerator not at the correct temperature—staff must fix it immediately.

Airports also have rules about cooking methods. They must handle grease disposal carefully so it does not cause a fire hazard or clog drains. Some places do not allow open flames in the terminal, so restaurants might use electric cooking equipment. Food waste is collected and disposed of properly to keep vermin away. All these steps help maintain a healthy environment in a busy place.

Duty-Free Shops and Taxes

International travelers often see "duty-free" shops after they pass passport control. These shops sell items without the usual taxes or duties, so they might be cheaper, especially for products like perfume, alcohol, or tobacco. However, not all travelers get a big discount—prices can vary. Duty-free rules differ from country to country. Sometimes you must show your boarding pass to prove you are traveling internationally before buying duty-free items.

Despite the name "duty-free," some countries or airports still charge local taxes. Or they might add them if you are traveling to certain destinations. You also have to consider your home country's rules on bringing items back. For example, there might be limits on how much alcohol or tobacco you can bring in without paying extra duty. It can be confusing, so travelers often read signs or ask the staff for details.

Other Retail Shops

Beyond duty-free, airports host a wide variety of stores. These can include:

- **Bookstores and Newsstands:** Selling books, magazines, newspapers, and small snacks.
- **Electronics Shops:** Offering headphones, chargers, cameras, and travel gadgets.

- **Clothing and Accessory Shops:** Sometimes big brands open airport branches for last-minute fashion needs or souvenirs.
- **Gift and Souvenir Shops:** Stocked with keychains, postcards, local crafts, and more.
- **Pharmacies and Health Stores:** Good for picking up medicine, vitamins, or personal care items you forgot to pack.

Some larger airports have high-end luxury boutiques that sell designer clothes, watches, or jewelry. They target international travelers who might have extra time or want to shop for luxury items at duty-free prices. Other airports focus more on practical needs, like travel pillows, eye masks, and luggage accessories. It depends on the airport's size, location, and the types of travelers who pass through.

Prices and Tips for Travelers

It is common for airport food or goods to be more expensive than outside. The businesses pay high rent to the airport and often must deal with the challenge of delivering supplies through security zones. If you want to save money, you can compare prices at different shops. A small convenience store might sell water or snacks cheaper than a sit-down café. Some airports also cap certain basic prices to keep them fair, so you might find that a bottle of water costs the same across all shops.

If you are traveling with your own water bottle, you can look for water fountains or bottle-filling stations to save on buying drinks. For food, you can sometimes bring your own snacks from home, as long as they pass security rules. Just remember that liquids and gels are restricted in carry-on bags, so large yogurt cups or drinks might be an issue.

Local Flair: Showcasing Regional Products

Many airports highlight their local culture and products. For example, if the region is famous for chocolates, there might be a gourmet chocolate shop. If it is known for craftsmanship, you might see a store selling handmade crafts or local art. Some airports have mini-exhibits or displays that teach visitors about local history or landmarks. This helps travelers get a sense of where they are, even if they are just passing through.

Airports might also invite local musicians or performers at certain times to entertain passengers. Although that is more about activities, it often happens in the same areas as shops and eateries. This creates a lively atmosphere and can make waiting more enjoyable.

Food Courts and Seating

In bigger airports, it is common to have a food court area where multiple restaurants and quick-serve stands cluster around a shared seating space. This arrangement is handy for groups who want different types of food but still want to sit together. Some food courts have large windows looking onto the tarmac, so you can watch planes come and go. You might also find charging outlets near tables, letting you power up devices while you eat.

During peak times, seating can become scarce. People try to find tables big enough for their luggage or choose spots near large windows for a good view. Some airports add extra standing counters for short-stay visitors who just want a quick bite. Others may have bright themes or decorative lighting to give the food court a friendly feel. The idea is to make the place comfortable and welcoming, since travelers might be tense or tired.

Special Dietary Options

Because people come from many backgrounds and have different preferences or restrictions, airports often aim to serve varied diets. You may find:

- **Vegetarian and Vegan Selections:** Salads, veggie burgers, or dishes made with plant-based ingredients.
- **Gluten-Free:** Wraps, cookies, or meals that do not include wheat or related grains.
- **Halal or Kosher:** In some airports, restaurants or packaged meals meet certain dietary requirements.
- **Allergy-Friendly:** Many eateries list common allergens, like nuts or dairy, to help people avoid them.

If you cannot find what you need, sometimes it is best to ask a staff member. They might point you to a special menu or brand that fits your dietary restrictions.

Lounges and Exclusive Dining

Some travelers have access to airline lounges because of their frequent flyer status or because they bought a ticket in a higher class of travel. These lounges often serve complimentary snacks, drinks, or even full meals. They might include quieter seating, faster Wi-Fi, and a relaxing environment away from the busy terminal. Though not shops or public eateries, lounges sometimes have buffets or bars.

If you do not have lounge access, you can sometimes pay a fee for entry. In that case, you get to enjoy the same free food and drinks, which can be worth it if you have a long layover. These lounges can be operated by airlines or by independent companies that let travelers in for a single visit or through a membership.

Managing Food Waste

Serving thousands of meals daily can create food waste. Airports and vendors try to reduce this by careful planning. If they know when peak traffic occurs, they can prepare just enough meals. Some airports donate unsold packaged foods to local charities, as long as it is allowed and safe. Others compost leftover scraps or recycle containers. In many terminals, you will see labeled bins for separating cans, paper, and organic waste. This helps keep waste out of landfills and supports sustainability.

How Airport Operators Choose Tenants

Airports sign contracts, known as concessions, with businesses that rent space. Potential tenants might go through a bidding process. If a famous coffee chain wants to open a store, they propose how much they will pay in rent and how they will design the space. The airport reviews bids and picks the ones that fit best, considering factors like brand reputation, expected sales, and variety for travelers. Over time, these deals might change, so the mix of shops and restaurants in a terminal can shift.

Some airports prefer to bring in local vendors to make the terminal feel unique. Others focus on well-known global chains for consistency. Many do a mix of both. The airport often sets rules about operating hours, menu offerings, and pricing to ensure travelers have a good experience.

Promotions, Events, and Seasonal Themes

To keep things interesting, airport shops and restaurants sometimes hold promotions. Around certain holidays, you might see festive decorations or special menu items. They may offer discounts on gifts or arrange pop-up shops showcasing local crafts. Sometimes, they organize small events, like cooking demos or product tastings, to attract travelers.

These promotions add to the airport's atmosphere. If you are waiting a long time, a small event or tasting booth can be a fun distraction. They might hand out samples, invite kids to decorate cookies, or display local art. For the businesses, it is a way to stand out among the many shops in the terminal.

Keeping Passengers Informed

With so many choices, travelers can become confused about where to eat or shop. That is why airports post maps, signs, and screens showing what is nearby. Some also have smartphone apps or interactive kiosks where you can search for specific items—like a phone charger or vegetarian food—and get directions to the relevant store or restaurant.

Gate announcements sometimes remind passengers that certain stores or food options are open. If a flight is delayed, travelers might have time for a sit-down meal. If it is an early morning flight, coffee shops might open extra early. The airport's communications team works with businesses to keep these details up to date.

Online Ordering and Delivery

In recent years, some airports introduced systems where you can order food online and have it delivered to your gate. You might scan a QR code posted on chairs or walls, see menus from various restaurants, and pay electronically. A runner brings your meal to you, saving you from standing in line. This can be handy if you need to stay close to your gate for an early boarding or if you have limited mobility.

Not all airports have this service, but it is growing. It can cut down on crowding in restaurants and give travelers more choice. However, there might be delivery fees or a limited range of menu items. The service also depends on staff availability. Even so, it is another example of how airports try to use technology to improve the passenger experience.

Children's Menus and Play Areas

Families traveling with kids often look for child-friendly meals or places to play. Some restaurants have kids' menus with smaller portions or simpler items like chicken nuggets or mac and cheese. They might also provide coloring sheets or crayons. Outside of the dining area, the airport could have a small play zone with soft flooring, slides, or toys. Parents might pick up a snack to enjoy while watching their children play. This setup can help everyone stay calm during a long wait.

Airport Shopping Beyond Basics

Large airports sometimes become destinations in themselves, with shops selling high-end clothing, jewelry, or electronics. In major hubs around the world, you can see entire rows of luxury boutiques. Some travelers like to shop for designer items they cannot find easily at home. Others might be in transit for many hours, so they welcome the chance to do some browsing.

At times, these bigger stores offer services like personal shopping, gift wrapping, or shipping purchases directly to your home address. They might also have exclusive products or regional specialties. While not every traveler wants to spend a lot of money during a layover, the variety can be interesting to explore.

Balancing Quiet and Busy Spaces

Some travelers like hustle and bustle—lots of shops and places to eat. Others prefer a quiet spot to rest or work. Airports try to balance these needs. They may group the shops and restaurants in one area, leaving some gates quieter. Seating away from the dining area can be calmer. This lets travelers who want peace and quiet find a restful corner, while those who enjoy the lively atmosphere can stay near the shops and eateries.

In some terminals, you will see quiet zones with comfortable chairs, small tables, or even reclining seats. Nearby, there might be only a coffee kiosk rather than a full-scale restaurant. The idea is to let people choose what kind of airport experience they want—social or serene.

Bringing It All Together

Eating and shopping at the airport might seem minor at first, but these services shape how travelers feel during their visit. A good meal can relieve stress and keep you satisfied until you get to your destination. A shop that sells essentials can save the day if you forgot an important item at home. Souvenir stands let you pick up last-minute gifts or mementos, and duty-free spots tempt you with special prices on perfumes or chocolates.

All these stores and restaurants also support the airport financially. They help pay for the operations that keep flights going—like runway maintenance, security, and improvements. The airport carefully chooses which businesses to include, aiming to meet the needs of a diverse group of travelers. They also watch for crowding, cleanliness, and local flavor to make the experience enjoyable.

When you pass through an airport, take a look around at the variety of places to eat and shop. You might try a local dish, find a handy gadget, or just enjoy a cup of coffee while watching planes move outside. It can turn waiting time into something relaxing or fun, creating a small break from the busy world of air travel.

CHAPTER 13: FIREFIGHTERS AT THE AIRPORT

When most people think of an airport, they imagine airplanes, runways, and terminals. But there is another group working at the airport, ready for serious events: the airport firefighters. These firefighters are different from the ones we see in towns and cities. They have special skills and gear, and they are prepared for airplane accidents, fuel spills, and other emergencies that can happen in and around an airfield. In this chapter, we will look at what airport firefighters do, the equipment they use, how they train, and why their work is so important.

Why Airports Need Their Own Firefighters

Air travel is safe, but planes carry many people and large amounts of fuel. If there is a problem, help must arrive immediately. Regular city fire stations might be too far to respond quickly. That is why airports often have their own fire stations, located near the runways. These stations are staffed 24 hours a day.

Airport firefighters handle a range of emergencies:

- **Airplane accidents or rough landings**
- **Fires on the runway or in airport buildings**
- **Fuel spills and leaks**
- **Medical emergencies**
- **People trapped or stuck in unusual places**
- **Problems with cargo that might catch fire or release smoke**

They are trained to handle special hazards, like burning jet fuel. Even if emergencies are rare, being ready can save lives and reduce damage.

The Fire Station on the Airfield

Most large airports have at least one dedicated fire station, sometimes more if the airfield is big. The station is usually close to the center of the runway system, so trucks can reach any part of the airfield fast. The building itself has large bays to store fire trucks, special foam trucks, and other rescue vehicles. It often has a control room where firefighters can track alarms, watch for weather warnings, and listen to radio updates.

Firefighters might live at or near the station in shifts. They have a kitchen, sleeping quarters, and places to rest so they are always on call. If the alarm sounds, they must rush to their vehicles and drive out immediately. Even at night, they can be in their trucks and out the door within seconds. The goal is to reach any part of the airport, including the farthest runway, in a very short time—often under three minutes.

Types of Firefighting Vehicles at Airports

Airport fire departments use specialized vehicles built to handle airplane fires and other airport dangers:

1. **ARFF Trucks (Aircraft Rescue and Fire Fighting Trucks)**
   These are large, sturdy vehicles with big water or foam tanks. They have turrets on top that can shoot foam or water far across the tarmac. Some have bumpers fitted with additional nozzles. ARFF trucks often have large, all-terrain tires to move over grass or uneven ground if a plane crashes off the runway.
2. **Rapid Intervention Vehicles**
   These are smaller, faster trucks that can reach an accident scene ahead of the bigger vehicles. They carry tools for quick rescue, such as cutters or spreaders to open jammed airplane doors. They might also have a smaller foam or water tank for immediate response.
3. **Water Tenders**
   Sometimes called tankers, these carry extra water to support the main ARFF trucks. If a runway fire lasts a long time, water tenders resupply the foam trucks so they do not have to leave the scene.
4. **Rescue Vans**
   These vans hold equipment for freeing trapped passengers, rope gear for heights, and medical supplies. They can also bring extra firefighters to the site.

Each truck is equipped with sirens, lights, radios, and thermal imaging cameras. Thermal imaging is helpful in heavy smoke or at night, because it can show the heat signature of fires or survivors.

How Airport Firefighters Fight Fuel Fires

Jet fuel is highly flammable. A small spark can start a dangerous fire. Airport firefighters use special foam designed to smother fuel flames by creating a blanket over the surface, cutting off oxygen. Water alone can make burning fuel spread, so foam is key. The foam is usually a mixture of water, a foam concentrate, and air. When pumped through the vehicle's turret, the foam lands on the fire, forming a thick layer that stops the flames.

Firefighters learn to position their trucks upwind of the fire—meaning they stay where the wind will not blow smoke and heat onto them. They also try to protect escape paths for passengers. If people are still inside a plane, rescuers aim to cool the aircraft's exterior, giving more time for evacuation. Some ARFF trucks can spray foam while moving, allowing them to approach the burning plane without risking the crew's safety.

Crash Rescue and Evacuation

When a plane makes an emergency landing or overruns the runway, firefighters respond with speed. Their first job is to assess the situation: Are there flames? Fuel leaks? Passengers trapped? They might approach the aircraft from different sides to control any fires and keep an exit route open.

Rescue operations often include:

- **Securing the area**: They block off the runway, keep other vehicles away, and confirm no other planes are landing or taxiing near the accident.
- **Cooling the plane's exterior**: If there is a fire, they direct foam or water onto the plane so passengers and crew can exit.
- **Opening doors or cutting through the fuselage**: If doors are jammed, firefighters have tools to cut or pry them open. Some doors might be stuck from a hard landing.
- **Assisting passengers**: Firefighters guide travelers away from the plane, provide first aid, and help anyone who has trouble walking. They also watch for hidden dangers, like collapsed landing gear or damaged wings that might drip fuel.

All of this must happen very fast, because smoke can fill a cabin quickly, and fire can spread.

Medical Response

Besides handling fires, airport firefighters often respond to medical calls. A passenger might collapse from a health issue, or a worker could get injured on the ramp. Many airport firefighters are trained as emergency medical technicians (EMTs) or paramedics. They carry equipment to handle:

- **Cardiac arrests**
- **Broken bones**
- **Cuts, burns, or smoke inhalation**
- **Allergic reactions**
- **Breathing problems**

They stabilize the patient and transfer them to an ambulance if needed. Because airports can be huge and confusing, having a dedicated medical response unit on site saves valuable minutes. Sometimes, if a flight crew declares a medical emergency mid-air, the airport team prepares an ambulance at the gate to help as soon as the plane lands.

Teamwork with Local Fire Departments

Airport fire services often cooperate with city or regional fire departments, especially if an event is large. For example, if an aircraft crashes outside the airport fence or hits buildings nearby, local firefighters might arrive as well. The airport team usually leads the way in controlling jet fuel fires because that is their specialty, but city departments bring extra manpower and vehicles.

They train together to learn each other's equipment and procedures. Some large cities have special agreements, so if the airport faces a big emergency, the city's resources can join in. In reverse, if the city has a large-scale fire, the airport may send certain vehicles to help, though they keep enough on hand in case something happens at the airport.

Daily Drills and Training

An airport firefighter's job demands constant practice. Drills can include:

- **Fire simulations**: The airport might have a training ground where they set controlled fires using mock airplane structures. Firefighters practice using foam, water, and rescue tools.

- **Evacuation drills**: They rehearse how to evacuate a plane with smoke machines creating a realistic scene. They learn how to guide passengers through the fastest exit route.
- **Vehicle operations**: Driving large ARFF trucks at high speed takes skill. Crews learn quick turns, braking, and off-road driving. They also practice using the turrets and hoses on the move.
- **Medical exercises**: Firefighters drill on treating wounds, performing CPR, and using defibrillators. They might practice carrying injured people out of a simulated wreck.
- **Hazardous materials (hazmat) drills**: Airports sometimes handle cargo with chemicals. Firefighters learn to spot leaks, contain spills, and protect themselves with hazmat suits.
- **Communication practice**: They work on radio calls and hand signals, so instructions are clear even in noisy, chaotic scenes.

These drills happen regularly. Some airports require big full-scale exercises every year or two, sometimes involving volunteer "victims," local hospitals, and air traffic control. After each exercise, they have meetings to see what worked and what needs improvement.

Protective Gear and Breathing Equipment

Airport firefighters wear gear that looks similar to city firefighters' suits, but often with extra protection against fuel fires. Standard parts include:

- **Fire-resistant coat and pants**: Made of special fabrics that shield from heat and flames.
- **Helmet with visor**: Protects the head from debris and intense heat.
- **Gloves and boots**: Thick material helps with heat, sharp edges, and slippery surfaces.
- **Self-contained breathing apparatus (SCBA)**: This tank and mask give them clean air so they are not breathing smoke or toxic fumes.

In major foam-dispensing operations, they might wear special chemical-resistant suits to guard against any chemicals in the foam or on the runway. Each piece of gear must be inspected often to ensure no tears or leaks. A small hole can let in toxic smoke or burn injuries.

Handling Fuel Spills and Other Hazards

A big threat at an airport is fuel leaks from airplanes or fuel trucks. A spill can spread across the tarmac, releasing fumes that could ignite. Firefighters have absorbent materials and special foam to cover spills. They also might use booms or barriers to contain the liquid so it does not run into drains or water sources. While they work, they keep sparks or open flames away, shutting down nearby equipment that could cause ignition.

Other hazards include battery fires in cargo, dangerous goods that might leak, or mechanical malfunctions in ground vehicles. Firefighters often carry portable extinguishers for smaller emergencies, and they coordinate with airport maintenance teams to handle the aftermath, like cleaning up the chemicals.

Fire Safety in the Terminal and Other Buildings

Besides the airfield, airport firefighters can respond to fires inside terminals, parking garages, hangars, or offices. These structures might have thousands of people inside. Smoke alarms, sprinkler systems, and fire doors help control flames, but if a fire does break out, the airport firefighters are first on scene.

They may need to evacuate a terminal, guide passengers through safe exits, and quickly put out the fire. The biggest challenge is the crowd. People might panic or be unsure where to go, so clear announcements and visible staff are vital. Firefighters and airport workers might direct travelers to assembly points away from the building. Afterward, they check for smoke damage and structural issues before letting flights resume as normal.

Protecting Cargo Facilities

Cargo facilities store goods that can be flammable, such as lithium batteries, chemicals, or compressed gases. If these catch fire, large and hot blazes can erupt. Firefighters at cargo buildings need knowledge of different packaging and shipping rules for hazardous materials. They keep reference guides that show how to handle each substance. For example, some chemicals react with water, so firefighters use dry powder or a specific type of foam instead. They also must keep an eye on ventilation, because smoke from certain chemicals can be toxic. Quick ventilation can help prevent explosions or build-up of harmful gases.

Working with Air Traffic Control

When an airplane declares an emergency, the air traffic control tower notifies the fire station immediately. Controllers tell firefighters which runway or area the plane is heading for, how serious the issue might be, and how many people are on board. Firefighters gather near the runway threshold, prepared to follow the plane as it lands. If the pilot reports a problem like hot brakes or engine trouble, firefighters watch the landing for signs of sparks or fire.

Once the plane stops, firefighters approach if needed, or stay a safe distance if everything is normal. If they see smoke, they rush in with foam lines ready. The tower also clears other planes away from that runway so the firefighters can work. Good communication between the tower and the fire station is essential, because every second counts.

Response Times and Airport Certification

A key measure for airport firefighters is how fast they can arrive where needed. Many aviation authorities have rules stating firefighters must reach the midpoint of each runway within a certain number of minutes. That is why stations and roads on the airfield are planned carefully.

Airports also want to keep a certain "level of protection," often labeled in categories based on the biggest airplane that uses the airport. Larger airplanes require more foam, more trucks, and more firefighters ready to respond. Authorities do routine checks, making sure the station meets these standards—enough staff, functioning trucks, foam reserves, and short response times.

Airport Firefighter Certification and Skills

People who want to become airport firefighters typically train as regular firefighters first. Then they get extra certificates in:

- **Aircraft Rescue and Fire Fighting (ARFF)**
- **Handling dangerous goods**
- **Operating high-capacity foam trucks**
- **Dealing with pressurized aircraft systems**

They might attend special ARFF schools where they practice with real airplane shells that can be set aflame in a controlled way. During training, they learn about airplane parts, such as fuel tanks, landing gear, cargo holds, and how to safely approach them. They also study the layout of their airport thoroughly. In an actual incident, knowing every taxiway and entrance helps them arrive faster.

Non-Emergency Duties and Fire Prevention

Between emergencies, airport firefighters still have many tasks:

- **Inspection tours**: They check hangars, fuel farms, and terminals to confirm sprinklers, hoses, and alarm systems are in good shape.
- **Fire safety education**: Sometimes they teach airport staff how to use fire extinguishers or handle small fires until the crew arrives.
- **Equipment checks**: Trucks and gear must be tested daily. They verify that foam levels are correct, hoses have no leaks, and engines run smoothly.
- **Records and training**: Firefighters log their activities, track how much foam or water is used, and study new rules about airport operations.

They also do smaller tasks like cleaning vehicles, stocking medical supplies, or practicing driving around updated runway routes if the airport does construction.

Large-Scale Drills with Other Agencies

In addition to daily or weekly drills, airports hold big exercises at least once every few years to test everyone's readiness for a major aircraft incident. During these exercises:

1. **Air traffic control** pretends a flight is in trouble, giving instructions as if it were real.
2. **Airport fire trucks** speed onto the runway. They practice spraying foam, rescuing dummy passengers, and coordinating with paramedics.
3. **Local hospitals** and ambulance services see how they would handle large groups of injured people.
4. **Police or security teams** handle crowd control, keep roads clear, and protect the crash site from unauthorized access.
5. **Volunteers** act as passengers, wearing makeup to show fake injuries so medical teams can practice triage.

Afterward, everyone meets to talk about what went well and what to improve. These drills keep all groups working together smoothly.

Dealing with Weather and Other Challenges

Fires do not wait for good weather. So airport firefighters must be prepared for rain, snow, strong winds, or even storms. Driving on a slippery runway is risky, especially if they have to aim a foam turret. The foam can freeze if temperatures are extremely low, so they might need to use heated trucks or special winter formulas. Heavy fog can also reduce visibility, making it harder to find a crash site.

They also face challenges like language barriers when helping international travelers. They must direct people who might not speak the local language. They might use simple hand signals or rely on flight attendants to translate. In all cases, quick thinking and calm action are vital.

Mental and Physical Fitness

Airport firefighters must stay physically strong. Their suits and gear are heavy, and climbing around a damaged plane can be tough. They lift and move equipment, sometimes rescuing injured people. Many departments require regular fitness tests, such as timed runs or strength tests.

The work can also be emotionally stressful. Though airplane accidents do not happen often, firefighters see serious or frightening events when they do. They might also handle medical calls where people are in pain or distress. Departments often provide mental health support or counseling. Being prepared mentally can help them stay focused and recover from stressful calls.

CHAPTER 14: WEATHER

The weather plays a big part in air travel. Bright, calm days make flights easier, while fog, storms, or high winds can cause delays and challenges. Airports and airlines pay close attention to changes in temperature, air pressure, wind direction, and more. In this chapter, we will explore how weather can shape the flying experience, how airports prepare, and what happens when nature does not cooperate.

Why Weather Matters for Airplanes

Airplanes rely on clear runways to take off and land. They also need stable air conditions in the sky. If there is ice on the wings, strong crosswinds, or poor visibility, it can become unsafe to fly. Pilots adjust flight routes, altitudes, or schedules based on the forecast. Air traffic controllers also space out planes more when storms or fog reduce visibility, leading to possible delays.

Key weather factors include:

- **Wind**: Impacts takeoffs and landings, especially crosswinds.
- **Rain, snow, or ice**: Affects runway grip and can hide runway markings.
- **Fog or low clouds**: Lowers visibility, making it harder to see the runway or other aircraft.
- **Thunderstorms**: Produce strong turbulence, lightning, and heavy rain or hail.
- **Temperature**: Very hot air is thinner, reducing an airplane's lift. Very cold weather can lead to icing.
- **Air pressure**: Changes how well engines perform and how instruments read altitude.

Pilots and controllers track these factors closely, deciding if and when it is safe to fly.

Wind and Runway Direction

Airports usually build runways to match the region's common wind patterns. Planes prefer to take off and land into the wind for better lift and control. If the wind changes direction, the control tower might switch to using another runway. This can be confusing for travelers who see flights land from one direction in the morning and the opposite way in the afternoon. But it is normal—it just reflects shifting winds.

Crosswinds can be a challenge. If the wind blows from the side, the pilot must angle the plane slightly to land straight on the runway. There is a limit to how strong a crosswind can be before it is unsafe. If it is too strong, the flight might divert to a different airport or wait for conditions to improve.

Rain and Wet Runways

Rain itself does not stop airplanes from flying, but it can make runways slippery and reduce visibility. Runway surfaces have grooves or a slight slope to help drain water. Even so, heavy rain might lead to standing water in some spots. Planes risk hydroplaning—when their tires lose contact with the ground due to a layer of water. Landing distance also becomes longer.

Pilots must factor in the wet surface when deciding their approach and speed. Air traffic controllers might leave extra space between landings if the runway is very wet, to avoid accidents. If rain is part of a storm, there might be strong wind gusts or lightning, adding more worry. Some airports experience monsoon seasons or heavy downpours, so they invest in good drainage systems to keep the runway as dry as possible.

Snow and Ice: Winter's Biggest Threats

In cold regions, snow and ice present serious risks. Aircraft wings must be free from ice, which disrupts airflow and reduces lift. Before takeoff, a plane might be sprayed with de-icing fluid to melt ice. If freezing rain or snow continues, anti-icing fluid can help keep ice from reforming for a short time. But the plane must take off soon after. If it waits too long, it may need another round of spraying.

On the ground, snowplows and brushes clear the runway. Workers spread de-icing chemicals to keep the pavement from icing over. If the snow falls faster than they can clear it, the runway might close temporarily. This can cause delays or canceled flights. Inside the terminal, travelers might see ongoing announcements about weather conditions and reasons for the closure. Despite the hassle, safety comes first, so planes do not attempt landings on dangerously slippery runways.

Fog and Low Visibility

Fog can form when air cools enough that water vapor condenses into tiny droplets. It is like a cloud at ground level. If fog is thick, pilots cannot see the runway or the lights until they are very close. Airports have special landing aids for low visibility:

- **ILS (Instrument Landing System)**: Sends signals to the plane's instruments, guiding it to the runway centerline and the correct descent angle.
- **Runway lights**: Bright approach and edge lights help the pilot align with the runway.
- **Ground radar**: Helps air traffic controllers monitor planes moving around in poor visibility.

If the fog is very dense, the airport might limit operations or suspend them. Planes waiting to land might hold in the air or divert. Departures might also wait if it is too risky to taxi around with almost zero visibility. Airports can upgrade to advanced systems—like Category III ILS—that allow landings in very low visibility, but that requires special pilot training and aircraft equipment.

Thunderstorms and Lightning

Thunderstorms produce heavy rain, strong winds, lightning, and sometimes hail or tornadoes. Planes do not take off or land if a thunderstorm is too close to the airport. Lightning can strike aircraft, though modern jets are built to handle lightning strikes by directing the electrical charge along the outer skin, but it is still dangerous to be on the ground fueling a plane when lightning is present. Workers on the ramp must stop fueling and other duties until the storm passes.

Windshear—a sudden change in wind speed or direction—is a big concern near thunderstorms. If a plane encounters windshear during takeoff or landing, the pilot needs fast reflexes to avoid a hard impact on the runway. Airports often have windshear detection systems that warn incoming flights. Pilots might go around or hold until the thunderstorm cell moves away.

Turbulence in the Air

Even if the weather at the airport is calm, planes can hit turbulence mid-flight. Turbulence happens when air currents move unpredictably, often near storms, mountains, or jet streams. It can range from light bumps to strong jolts that cause drinks to spill or unbuckled passengers to bounce around. Pilots try to avoid known areas of severe turbulence by flying around storms or changing altitude. Air traffic controllers help them find smoother air if possible.

Turbulence can rattle nerves, but modern aircraft are built to withstand it. Passengers should keep seat belts fastened whenever seated. Cabin crew might pause food service during bad turbulence, and the pilot might make an announcement urging everyone to sit down and buckle up. Once the plane passes through or around the rough patch, it often returns to a smooth ride.

Very Hot Weather

In hot conditions, air density is lower. Thin air means planes need more runway to achieve the same lift. You might notice flights restricted on extremely hot days. For example, if the temperature is above a certain limit, the pilot might reduce the plane's load—meaning fewer passengers or less cargo—or wait until it cools off. Airports at high altitudes can face this problem more often. In some desert locations, summer temperatures exceed airplane limits if flights occur at midday. Airlines may schedule flights for early morning or late evening instead.

Hot weather also puts stress on ground systems and vehicles. Engines can overheat, and asphalt on runways might soften slightly, though modern runway materials help reduce this risk. Ramp workers need water and shade to prevent heat exhaustion. Despite the heat, flights can run safely if the airline adjusts flight plans for the thinner air.

Extreme Cold and Frozen Equipment

In very cold areas, metal parts on planes can become brittle if not designed for sub-zero conditions. Ground vehicles might have trouble starting. Workers wear thick clothing, but that can slow down their tasks. De-icing fluid must be mixed properly to prevent freezing. If an airport is far north, it likely invests in heated hangars, specialized vehicles, and robust runways that handle deep frost. Even then, extremes of weather can cause closures.

When temperatures drop below a certain point, aircraft might need to remain plugged into ground power to keep instruments warm. Fuel can become thick in extreme cold, so airlines store planes in heated facilities overnight if possible. If that is not possible, they run the engines occasionally or keep special heaters near the plane's parts.

Tropical Storms and Hurricanes

In tropical regions, hurricanes or cyclones can bring heavy rain, strong winds, and flooding. Airports may close in advance if a hurricane is forecast to hit. Airlines fly planes to safer airports so they are not stuck or damaged. Terminal windows may be boarded up or reinforced. After the storm passes, the airport checks runways for debris or flooding.

Sometimes, an airport can reopen quickly, helping bring relief flights with food, medicine, or rescue teams. But if the storm damage is large, it might take days or weeks to repair. Hangars can lose roofs, runway lighting can fail, and communications might be down. Planning for hurricane season is a major part of airports in coastal areas. They often have emergency generators and extra supplies to weather the storm and recover fast.

Volcanoes and Ash Clouds

Volcanic eruptions can send ash high into the sky. This ash is not just dust—it is made of tiny, sharp bits of rock and glass. If a plane's engines ingest ash, it can damage the turbines, leading to engine failure. That is why flights avoid volcanic ash clouds at all costs.

Airports far from a volcano can still suffer if wind carries ash over them. Flights might be canceled or rerouted for days. One famous example happened some years ago when a volcano erupted, and ash spread across parts of Europe, grounding thousands of flights. Airports and meteorological offices track ash clouds carefully. Pilots get alerts on their route to avoid danger zones.

Weather Forecasting at Airports

Airports depend on detailed weather reports to plan operations. They have:

1. **Meteorological offices**: Some airports have an on-site weather station with meteorologists. They release weather balloons, track radar images, and share forecasts with air traffic control and airlines.
2. **Automated weather observing systems (AWOS or ASOS)**: These machines measure wind speed, temperature, pressure, visibility, and cloud height. They send this data to controllers, pilots, and forecast centers.
3. **Runway sensors**: Detect runway temperature, friction levels, and if there is any icing.
4. **Pilot reports (PIREPs)**: Pilots share real-time weather details while in flight—like turbulence, icing, or cloud layers. These help others plan.

By gathering this data, airports can announce conditions like "wind 10 knots from the east, visibility 2 miles in rain," or "heavy snow, runway closed." Pilots read these notices before takeoff or landing, adjusting their approach as needed.

How Controllers and Pilots Make Decisions

When weather is poor, air traffic controllers might:

- **Space out arrivals and departures more**: So planes have more time to land safely.
- **Assign alternate runways**: If the wind changed direction or one runway is being cleared of snow.
- **Hold planes at the gate**: If the conditions are too risky.

Pilots also make choices:

- **Divert to another airport**: If storms or fog make landing unsafe.
- **Delay departure**: If severe weather is expected en route or at the destination.
- **Adjust speed or altitude**: Climb above a storm system or go around it.

These measures might frustrate passengers with long delays, but they ensure safety. No pilot wants to land blindly in a severe storm, and controllers must keep the airspace organized.

Dealing with Frequent Weather Changes

Weather can shift quickly—one minute it is clear, the next, a thunderstorm forms. Airports keep a constant watch with radar and satellite data, plus local observations. If conditions deteriorate, ground crews might rush to move vehicles and planes to safer spots. If lightning is near, fueling stops at once. If hail threatens, planes might be moved into hangars if there is time, though that is not always possible.

Sometimes a big airport can stay partly open while a storm affects only one side of the field. Then controllers route planes to runways on the clearer side. They balance the changing weather against flight schedules, usually with real-time updates to the airlines and flight crews.

Climate Differences Around the World

Airports around the globe face various climate challenges:

- **In desert areas**, extreme heat, sandstorms, or dust devils might disrupt operations.
- **In polar regions**, constant ice, snow, and freezing temperatures require special gear year-round.
- **In tropical zones**, heavy rain, high humidity, and storms can be daily issues.
- **In mountainous areas**, the wind can shift rapidly, creating turbulence or downdrafts. Pilots and controllers must be extra cautious.

Each airport invests in the right tools for its local weather, such as advanced snowplows in cold places or improved drainage in rainy environments. Crews train specifically for what is most common, but they also keep some readiness for rare surprises, like an unusual hailstorm in a warm region.

Technology Helping Weather Tracking

Modern technology helps airports manage weather better:

- **Doppler radar**: Detects wind patterns and precipitation, picking up rotation in storm clouds that can signal tornadoes or microbursts.
- **Satellite imagery**: Shows large weather systems, like hurricanes or wide storm fronts.
- **Computer models**: Forecasters use them to predict changes in wind, temperature, or storms hours or days ahead.

- **Lightning detection networks**: Pinpoint where lightning strikes, warning ramp crews to stop fueling.
- **Weather apps and digital boards**: Let passengers and staff see minute-by-minute updates, so they can plan.

Airports share this data with pilots and airline dispatchers, who then map the safest flight path. This technology reduces last-second surprises, though weather can still do unexpected things.

Storm Shelters and Airport Safety for Passengers

If a severe storm hits while you are in the terminal, the airport might have a plan to move everyone away from windows or into protected hallways. In tornado-prone areas, airports sometimes designate interior rooms as tornado shelters. Strong winds can break glass or toss debris around the apron. Announcements over the PA system tell travelers what to do, and airport staff guide them if an evacuation is needed. While such events are not common, the airport's emergency plans cover these situations for everyone's safety.

Keeping Runways Clear Around the Clock

Many large airports operate day and night. If a snowstorm arrives at 3 a.m., the snow removal teams must be there, clearing the runways and taxiways to be ready for morning flights. If a hurricane hits in the middle of the night, staff might close the airport but still remain on-site or close by to begin post-storm cleanup as soon as it is safe. Weather does not follow business hours, so airports often have rotating shifts of workers, always on duty to handle changes.

Passenger Tips for Weather-Related Delays

Though we want to avoid repeating advice given in earlier chapters, here are a few fresh suggestions specific to weather:

1. **Check the forecast for both your departure and destination**: If storms are expected, consider arriving at the airport earlier, since lines might be long or flights might change.
2. **Sign up for airline alerts**: Airlines often send messages if a flight is delayed or canceled because of weather.
3. **Pack items in carry-on**: If you end up stuck overnight, you have necessities like medication, a phone charger, and perhaps a change of clothes with you.

4. **Stay near the gate**: In fast-changing weather, a short break in the storm might allow a plane to depart quickly. If you wander too far, you could miss the call to board.
5. **Stay patient**: Nobody controls the weather, and safety is the top concern. Venting frustration may not speed things up.

These steps help you cope with weather disruptions. Airports and airlines work hard to keep travelers informed.

The Ongoing Challenge of Weather

Even with modern tools and skilled staff, weather will always be a big factor in air travel. It can appear out of nowhere, force pilots to divert, or cause ground crew to stop working temporarily. Each airport has its own climate challenges, from snow to tropical storms. While these conditions can be frustrating for travelers, they are an unavoidable part of flying.

In the end, focusing on safety matters most. Airlines, pilots, and air traffic controllers continually adapt to changing weather data, making decisions to protect the people on board. Airport ground crews respond by clearing runways, de-icing planes, and looking after passengers stuck in the terminal. Over time, improvements in weather forecasting, radar, and airplane technology have made it easier to handle storms, fog, or heat. But a big part of flying remains cooperating with nature and learning to expect that, sometimes, the sky has other plans.

CHAPTER 15: MOVING GOODS BY AIR

Airports are not just about moving people. They are also important centers for moving goods. Many of the products we see in stores—like fresh fruits, electronics, or even urgent medical supplies—often travel by plane. This type of shipping is known as air cargo. Because airplanes are fast, they can move items around the world in a shorter amount of time than ships or trucks. In this chapter, we will look at how cargo moves through airports, who is involved, and why air transport is so vital for global business.

Why Ship by Air?

Air cargo offers a major benefit: speed. When items are shipped by sea, they might take weeks to get from one continent to another. Airplanes can do the same trip in a day or less. For businesses that need to deliver products quickly, or for those shipping fresh or time-sensitive goods, air transport is the top choice. Examples include:

- **Fresh produce**: Fruits, vegetables, or flowers that could spoil if shipped slowly.
- **Medical supplies**: Urgent items like organs for transplant, vaccines, or other medications that must arrive quickly.
- **High-value electronics**: Laptops, cell phones, or parts needed for production lines.
- **Emergency relief supplies**: During disasters, cargo planes carry food, tents, or rescue equipment to hard-to-reach places.

Although air cargo is more expensive than shipping by sea, it is the best option when time is crucial or the goods are valuable.

The Types of Aircraft Used for Cargo

1. **Dedicated Freighters**
   Some planes are built or converted specifically for carrying cargo. These have wide doors and empty main decks with tracks for containers or pallets. They may lack passenger windows or seats and have stronger

floors to handle heavy loads. Examples include large freighter versions of popular aircraft, such as the Boeing 747F or Boeing 777F.

2. **Passenger Planes (Belly Cargo)**
Even planes carrying passengers often have space in the "belly," the lower deck below the passenger cabin. Airlines use this space to load extra cargo, usually in containers that fit alongside checked luggage. This is called belly cargo. It is common to find boxes, mail sacks, or smaller shipments traveling beneath your feet when you fly.

3. **Combi Aircraft**
A few airlines operate combi planes with part of the cabin for passengers and part for cargo. There might be a partition in the cabin, and large freight doors for loading items. This setup is less common now but can be useful in regions with less demand for passengers but higher need for cargo.

4. **Small Planes**
In remote areas, small propeller-driven planes might deliver goods like mail, medicines, or food to towns without road access. These planes may land on short or unpaved runways. Their cargo space is limited, but they can bring essential items to distant places.

Cargo Handling at the Airport

The process of moving cargo at airports involves several steps:

1. **Receiving and Inspection**
Goods arrive at a cargo terminal or warehouse. Workers check the paperwork, weigh the shipment, and inspect the packaging. They also confirm that the items match what the sender declared. If the goods are perishable, like flowers or produce, they might be stored in coolers until loading time.

2. **Security Screening**
Just like passenger baggage, cargo must be screened to ensure nothing dangerous is onboard. This can involve x-ray machines or special sniffing equipment that detects explosives. Large crates might be opened for a manual check or scanned with advanced imaging technology.

3. **Unitizing (Building Up) Shipments**
Many airports use Unit Load Devices (ULDs). A ULD is like a large container or a sturdy pallet with walls. Workers load boxes or packages

into a ULD, then secure it with nets or locking panels. Each container is labeled with a barcode or tag that shows where it is going. Using ULDs helps speed up loading and unloading, because the whole container can be moved in or out of the plane with a specialized loader.

4. **Storage and Ramp Transfer**
   After the ULDs are prepared, they are stored briefly in a secure area until the flight is ready. Then ground vehicles, like cargo tractors, pull the containers to the aircraft. For large freighters, an elevated cargo loader lifts the ULDs to the plane's door. Workers push or roll them along built-in tracks until they lock into place. The cargo hold is arranged carefully so the plane's weight is balanced.

5. **Transport and Arrival**
   Once the plane lands, the process happens in reverse. The cargo is offloaded, cleared through customs, and picked up by trucks or smaller vehicles for final delivery. If it is an international shipment, customs officials check to make sure all import rules are met, and any applicable duties are paid.

Types of Goods Moved by Air

Not all goods are suitable for plane transport, but plenty are:

- **Perishables**: Fruits, vegetables, meat, fish, flowers, and dairy. These often go in temperature-controlled containers or coolers.
- **Pharmaceuticals**: Medicines may need stable temperatures to remain effective. Cargo operators use "cool chain" logistics to keep them within the right temperature range.
- **High-Value Items**: Jewelry, electronics, or fashion goods can be shipped by air to reduce the risk of theft or damage over long sea voyages.
- **Spare Parts**: For companies with factories worldwide, an unexpected breakdown might need a replacement part in hours, not weeks. Air freight is ideal here.
- **Mail and Parcels**: Postal services use cargo flights to move letters and packages across big distances quickly. Companies like express couriers also rely heavily on air networks.
- **Live Animals**: From racehorses to pets and zoo animals, specialized cargo planes can carry them, using climate-controlled and secure enclosures.

Perishable Shipments and Temperature Control

Moving fresh goods like fruit or fish requires special attention. If these items get too warm or too cold, they can spoil. Cargo planes or ULDs may have temperature controls, like built-in refrigeration. Workers place temperature sensors in crates to ensure conditions stay correct during flight. Some shipments might use dry ice or gel packs to keep items cool. Airports with a large amount of perishable cargo have refrigerated warehouses or "cool rooms." As soon as the goods arrive, they are transferred there until the plane is ready. This reduces the time items spend in warm or humid conditions on the tarmac.

Pharmaceuticals can be even stricter. Certain vaccines or drugs might only be stable within a tight temperature window. If conditions are not met, the shipment becomes useless. So cargo handlers follow "cold chain" protocols, carefully logging temperatures at each stage. If the temperature strays from the required range, the shipment might need to be inspected or discarded for safety.

Speed vs. Cost: Balancing Factors

While air cargo is fast, it can be costly. Airlines charge by weight or volume, whichever is higher. A bulky yet lightweight item might cost more if it occupies a lot of space. Businesses must decide if the speed justifies the expense. For high-value products, the extra cost is acceptable since the items can sell quickly upon arrival. For fresh foods, arriving fast means better quality on store shelves. But for lower-value, bulky goods, shipping by ocean remains cheaper.

Additionally, some companies use a mix. Urgent or fragile items go by plane, while larger or less time-sensitive items go by ship. This approach helps manage costs while still meeting deadlines. Many logistics companies help plan these strategies, tracking shipments from factory to store.

Customs and Border Checks

When cargo crosses international borders, airports have customs officers who verify each shipment. They check documents like the Air Waybill (the cargo version of a passenger ticket), commercial invoices, and details about the product's origin. If the shipment is restricted—say, a special chemical or animal product—extra permits may be needed.

In some countries, cargo can be "bonded," meaning it stays in a special warehouse without paying import taxes immediately. Then it might be sent on another flight to a different country. Free trade zones at airports also allow cargo to be processed more easily before it moves on. All these measures keep track of items so that governments know what enters or leaves their territory.

Dangerous Goods Regulations

Certain products are called "dangerous goods" or "hazardous materials." Examples include:

- **Flammable liquids** (paint, some cleaning agents)
- **Gases** (compressed oxygen, aerosols)
- **Corrosives** (battery acid)
- **Explosives** (fireworks)
- **Radioactive items** (medical isotopes)

These goods can still ship by air under strict rules. They must be packaged according to international standards, clearly labeled, and declared. The pilot needs to know what is onboard in case of an emergency. If misdeclared or incorrectly packed, these materials pose huge risks. Some airlines have special teams to handle dangerous goods, double-checking each container for safety compliance.

Courier and Express Shipments

Companies like FedEx, UPS, or DHL built global networks using cargo planes. They run massive sorting hubs at certain airports (like Memphis for FedEx or Louisville for UPS). Here, thousands of packages arrive by plane, get sorted on conveyor belts, and quickly reload onto other planes going to final destinations. This "hub and spoke" model means packages can travel from many origins to many places through one or two central hubs.

If you send an express package, it might leave your local pickup point in a truck, transfer to a nearby airport, and then board a cargo plane to the sorting hub. After a quick re-sort, it boards another plane heading closer to the destination, then finishes the trip by truck. This entire process can happen overnight, allowing next-day delivery across continents.

The Rise of E-Commerce

Online shopping has exploded in recent years, creating an even bigger demand for air cargo. People can order items from another country and expect delivery in a few days. Airlines and airports had to adjust, handling a surge in small parcels. E-commerce giants might charter entire planes for busy shopping seasons or set up their own air fleets. For example, some major online retailers operate their own planes to handle the volume of orders.

Smaller businesses can also tap into this global network, selling handmade goods or specialty products to distant markets. With quick shipping, they can promise faster delivery times, though shipping costs can be high. Consumers like the convenience of receiving items fast, so e-commerce is a major force pushing cargo growth.

Airport Infrastructure for Cargo

Many airports have separate cargo terminals far from passenger terminals. These zones are bigger, with space for trucks, warehouses, refrigeration units, sorting belts, and areas for animals or hazardous goods. Wide taxiways allow large freighter planes to park and load. Some busy cargo airports have multiple ramps dedicated to specific cargo airlines. Others might have combined facilities for several carriers.

Good road access is vital, because cargo must move quickly to or from the airport. Cargo terminals often link to highways or major roads. Some also connect to rail lines, improving efficiency for longer land transport. Automated systems in warehouses can scan and move packages on conveyor belts, speeding up sorting. All these features let airports handle thousands of tons of goods daily.

Special Handling for Live Animals

Shipping live animals by plane takes extra care. Horses, for example, travel in sturdy "horse stalls" that fit inside cargo planes. Grooms or caretakers might fly along to feed and calm the animals. Zoos might move exotic creatures in climate-controlled crates, with special lighting or ventilation. Pets can also fly as cargo if they are too large for the passenger cabin, though many owners prefer to keep smaller pets with them.

During the flight, the cargo hold must keep a stable temperature, and the animals need enough space to stand or lie down comfortably. Airline staff check on them at stops. Some airports have "animal lounges" or holding facilities where animals can rest, get food or water, and be inspected by a vet before continuing. Proper documentation is needed, including health certificates and import permits, especially for endangered species.

Charter Cargo Flights

Sometimes a company needs to move a large or unusual item, like an entire factory machine or a massive piece of artwork. They might hire a cargo charter. This is a plane booked just for that shipment, with a schedule set by the customer. Charter flights can also be arranged for emergency deliveries. For example, if a power plant part fails, the factory might charter a plane to deliver the replacement overnight and avoid extended shutdown.

Heavy-lift planes, like the Antonov An-124 or An-225, can carry extremely large loads. They have ramps that allow vehicles or huge machinery to roll aboard. These planes can land at airports with suitable runways that can handle their weight. When large infrastructure projects happen—like building an oil field in a remote spot—cargo charters bring in equipment not feasible to move any other way.

Security and Theft Prevention

High-value cargo is tempting for thieves. Airports and cargo operators use many security measures:

- **Fenced and monitored cargo areas**: Guards, cameras, and controlled entry gates.
- **Tracking and sealing**: Each container might have a seal that shows if it was tampered with, and a barcode or RFID tag to track location.
- **Background checks**: Workers who handle valuable shipments undergo checks, ensuring they do not have a history of theft.
- **Secured vehicles**: When trucks move high-value cargo, they might have GPS tracking or travel in convoys with escorts.

Airlines follow national and international rules for cargo screening. They check for hidden items that could pose a risk to flight safety. Sometimes shipments are "known shipper" verified, meaning the sender is trusted and has a record of safe shipments.

Green Initiatives in Air Cargo

Air freight can have a larger carbon footprint per kilogram than sea or ground transport, mainly because planes burn more fuel. However, steps are being taken to reduce environmental impact:

- **Fuel-efficient planes**: New models, like certain twin-engine jets, burn less fuel than older freighters.
- **Improved loading efficiency**: By filling planes closer to capacity and using lighter materials for containers, carriers can reduce fuel burn per pound of cargo.
- **Sustainable aviation fuels**: Some airlines are testing biofuels or synthetic blends, which can lower carbon emissions.
- **Optimized routing**: Computer systems help plan flight paths to avoid extra miles or extended waiting in the air.

Shippers also might use carbon offset programs. However, the main advantage of air cargo remains speed, so environmental solutions must balance timeliness with reduced fuel use.

How Airports Grow Cargo Business

Many airports see cargo as a way to expand revenue. They advertise their location, low fees, or modern facilities to attract cargo airlines. If an airport sits near major highways or population centers, it can be a strong distribution point. They might build bigger warehouses or partner with logistics companies for custom solutions.

Some airports also host trade shows, inviting logistics experts to see their cargo terminals and learn about new developments. By offering incentives, such as reduced landing fees for freighters or guaranteed night slots, they encourage airlines to choose that airport for cargo operations. This competition can be fierce, especially between hubs trying to dominate cargo routes in a region.

Challenges in Air Cargo

Despite the advantages, air cargo faces:

- **High costs**: Not all goods can afford the premium.
- **Limited capacity**: Belly cargo might rely on passenger flights. When passenger traffic drops (for example, during global events or slow travel periods), available cargo space also shrinks.
- **Infrastructure limits**: Some airports do not have large enough warehouses, or the runways might be too short for big cargo jets.
- **Regulations**: International rules can be complex, including environmental laws, customs duties, and transport of restricted items.
- **Delays and congestion**: Busy airports can have ramp congestion, leading to missed connections or slower processing.

However, demand for quick deliveries keeps the cargo sector growing overall. Innovation in packaging, digital tracking, and scheduling helps reduce some challenges.

Digital Tracking and Paperless Systems

Technology simplifies many steps:

- **E-AWB (Electronic Air Waybill)**: Replaces paper forms, speeding up customs clearance.
- **Real-time shipment tracking**: Cargo owners can see where their goods are, from the warehouse to the airplane and beyond.
- **Electronic customs filings**: Speeds up border checks, reducing waiting times.
- **Smart sensors**: Some containers or packages have trackers that measure temperature, humidity, or vibrations during transit. If something goes out of range, operators get alerts.

These improvements reduce errors in paperwork, help find issues quickly, and give customers more confidence in air freight services.

Future Trends in Air Cargo

1. **Drones and Small UAVs**
   In remote or crowded cities, delivery drones may carry small parcels.

While they are limited in distance and weight, they could fill a niche for last-mile deliveries from the airport to final destinations.

2. **Automation and Robots**

   Warehouses might use autonomous vehicles to move cargo around, or robotic arms to load containers. This can boost speed and reduce the need for manual labor, though skilled operators will still be needed to oversee the systems.

3. **Dedicated Cargo Hubs**

   As e-commerce keeps expanding, more airports might become specialized cargo hubs. Airlines could schedule flights purely around shipping demands, not passenger timetables.

4. **Shorter International Supply Chains**

   Some companies, aiming to cut costs or manage risk, might shift production closer to buyers. However, fast shipments will still be key for urgent or specialized products, ensuring that air cargo remains in demand.

5. **New Aircraft Designs**

   Future cargo planes might use electric or hybrid engines for short routes, or incorporate advanced materials to reduce weight. While large battery-powered freighters are not yet common, research is ongoing.

CHAPTER 16: HELPING PEOPLE WITH DIFFERENT NEEDS

Airports welcome travelers from every walk of life. Some passengers might have disabilities or need special assistance, while others could be traveling with young children or might not speak the local language. Many airports have programs, staff, and facilities to help these individuals navigate the terminal safely and comfortably. In this chapter, we will learn how airports address different needs, from providing wheelchairs to ensuring clear signage. By focusing on accessibility and support, airports aim to serve all travelers with respect.

Why Accessibility and Support Matter

Millions of people use airports each day, including seniors, individuals with visual or hearing differences, travelers with limited mobility, families with infants, and more. If an airport were not set up for diverse needs, a large group of travelers could struggle to check in, pass security, or board flights. By creating an accessible environment, airports:

- **Reduce stress for everyone**: A well-designed space makes air travel smoother for all.
- **Comply with laws**: Many countries have regulations that require public places to be accessible.
- **Build a positive reputation**: When travelers have good experiences, they are more likely to return or recommend the airport.
- **Promote inclusion**: People with disabilities can travel more freely, removing barriers that once limited their mobility or independence.

Mobility Assistance: Wheelchairs and More

One of the most common forms of assistance is helping travelers with limited mobility. Airlines often provide wheelchairs for passengers who ask for them during booking or check-in. Airport staff can escort these travelers from the check-in desk through security and to their gate. In some places, staff with specialized training operate powered carts or electric buggies that carry multiple passengers at once.

If the flight uses a jet bridge, pushing a wheelchair onto the plane is straightforward. For smaller planes or remote stands, lifts or portable ramps can help. Some airports have "ambulifts"—vehicles that raise a small cabin to the airplane's door, allowing wheelchair users to board without climbing stairs.

Low Vision or Blind Travelers

For travelers who have partial or no sight, airports incorporate features to help them move around:

- **Braille or Tactile Signs**: Elevator buttons, restroom signs, or floor maps might include braille labels.
- **Audible Announcements**: Gates or flight changes are often announced over loudspeakers. Some airports also have interactive audio guidance to direct travelers to gates or exits.
- **Guided Assistance**: Staff or volunteers can guide a blind traveler by the arm, describing the path or reading signs.
- **Tactile Pathways**: Some terminals have floor markings that a traveler can detect with a cane, guiding them to important areas.

People with guide dogs can bring their animals into the terminal and, in many countries, onto the plane. Airports might offer relief areas where service animals can drink water or use a patch of grass or special mat.

Deaf or Hard-of-Hearing Passengers

Clear communication is essential. Travelers who are deaf or have reduced hearing can benefit from:

- **Visual Flight Information Displays**: Large screens that show flight times, gate numbers, and any updates. These screens often repeat announcements like gate changes.
- **Captioning on Monitors**: Some airports add real-time captions to important announcements on TV screens in waiting areas.
- **Video Relay Services**: If a deaf traveler needs to communicate with staff, some terminals have kiosks or apps that connect to a sign-language interpreter.

- **Vibrating Pagers or Apps**: Certain airlines offer devices or phone app notifications that vibrate when boarding starts or if there is a gate change.

Staff might also have basic skills for simple sign language or they rely on notes and gestures. This ensures that a traveler who cannot hear announcements can still get the information they need.

Intellectual or Developmental Differences

People with cognitive or developmental differences, such as autism, dementia, or Down syndrome, may need extra assistance. Airports and airlines can help by:

- **Offering Simulation Visits**: Some airports let families come on a quieter day to practice the check-in and security process. This helps reduce anxiety when the real flight happens.
- **Providing a Quiet Room**: A calm space with low lighting and fewer people helps if someone feels overwhelmed by the noisy, busy terminal.
- **Trained Staff**: Employees might learn how to communicate using simple language, be patient with repeated questions, or help manage sensory overload.
- **Clear Signage and Symbols**: Simple, easy-to-understand signs can guide travelers who might not read well or who need visual cues.

In some locations, travelers can request a special wristband or lanyard that discreetly signals to staff they might need extra time or direct guidance. This helps staff identify who needs support without the traveler having to explain in detail each time.

Traveling with Young Children

Parents with babies or small kids can face several challenges:

1. **Strollers and Baby Gear**
   Many airports allow strollers right up to the gate. Then they are gate-checked, meaning they will be stowed in the cargo hold and often returned at the airplane door upon landing.
2. **Changing Stations**
   Restrooms typically have fold-down changing tables. Some airports go

further, providing family restrooms with extra space and sinks at a child's height.

3. **Play Areas**
   To burn off energy, kids can visit play zones with soft mats or small slides. These zones keep children entertained and give parents a break while waiting for boarding.
4. **Children's Menus**
   In the terminal's restaurants, some places offer smaller, simpler meals for kids. If children are picky eaters, parents might pack snacks or get something from a shop inside the airport.

Staff can also help parents who are juggling luggage and kids, especially if they need to board early or navigate a busy terminal. An airline might call families first during boarding, letting them settle in before the rush.

Language Assistance

Airports see travelers from many countries. Signs often appear in multiple languages, such as English plus the local language. Major hubs might include additional languages, like Chinese, Spanish, or French. Beyond signs:

- **Translation or Interpretation**
  Large airports might have information desks staffed by multilingual personnel. They can answer questions or point travelers to the correct gate. Some airlines hire staff with different language skills at check-in.
- **Technology and Apps**
  If no staff are available who speak a certain language, phone apps with instant text or voice translation can bridge the gap. Some airports install digital kiosks that provide instructions in various languages.
- **Symbols and Icons**
  Universal icons for restrooms, exits, baggage, or lost-and-found help travelers even if they cannot read the text. Arrows and color-coded lines on floors can guide them to important areas.

By removing language barriers, airports lower confusion for tourists and business visitors alike.

Medical Needs and Hidden Disabilities

Not all conditions are visible. Some travelers might have breathing problems, heart issues, or chronic pain that is not obvious. They might need:

- **Oxygen or Medical Equipment**
  If a traveler needs supplemental oxygen, they must arrange it with the airline in advance. Airports usually allow small oxygen tanks or concentrators through security if they meet airline rules. Some passengers also use wearable medical devices that should not pass through x-ray scanners, so they ask for a pat-down instead.
- **Seating for Physical Discomfort**
  Those with back pain or arthritis might need extra rest or prefer to board early. Some terminals supply special seating with extra padding or recliners in quiet corners.
- **Medication Storage**
  People carrying medicines that need refrigeration might store them in an insulated bag. If the layover is long, an airport lounge or medical facility might help keep them cool. Security officers usually permit medicines in carry-on if the traveler has the correct prescriptions.
- **Invisible Disabilities Lanyards**
  Some airports adopt a system where travelers can wear a green lanyard with sunflowers or a similar symbol indicating they have a hidden disability. Staff are trained to notice and offer help if the traveler seems confused or stressed.

Service Animals and Emotional Support Animals

We discussed guide dogs, but there are also hearing dogs or service animals trained to do tasks for individuals with mobility differences. Many airports let them accompany passengers in the terminal, but different airlines have different rules about which animals can travel in the cabin. Some used to allow emotional support animals, but policies have changed in many places. Now they often require these animals to travel as pets if they do not meet strict service-animal guidelines.

Airports might have relief areas indoors or outdoors where animals can relieve themselves. They often include fake grass, a fire hydrant prop, and waste bags.

Signs direct travelers with service animals to these areas. Staff may also show them if the passenger requests assistance.

Priority Lines and Pre-Boarding

Travelers needing extra assistance typically appreciate shorter lines or designated lanes at check-in, security, or immigration. Some examples:

- **Special Lanes at Security**
  If someone has trouble standing for long, the airport might direct them to a faster lane. Some families with young kids or strollers also get a separate lane to handle liquids, formula, or baby food easily.
- **Pre-Boarding**
  Airlines often invite travelers with disabilities, seniors, or families with very young kids to board before general passengers. This helps them find seats without feeling rushed or dealing with crowded aisles.
- **Express Immigration Lanes**
  In certain countries, a traveler with a disability might receive a special pass to go through immigration more quickly. However, this depends on local regulations.

While priority lines speed up the process, staff also need to balance fairness. Some passengers might try to misuse these lanes. Hence, airports might ask for documentation if the disability is not apparent.

Staff Training for Sensitivity and Respect

Airports that care about accessibility invest in staff training:

- **Disability Awareness**
  Employees learn about different conditions, from autism to limited mobility. They practice how to communicate in a respectful, clear way, such as asking, "How may I help you?" instead of making assumptions.
- **Proper Use of Mobility Aids**
  Staff are taught how to push wheelchairs or operate lifts carefully. They should ask permission before touching someone's equipment or service animal.

- **Avoiding Patronizing Language**
  They avoid speaking to an adult with a disability as if addressing a child. Staff do not take control away from the traveler unless safety is at stake.
- **Handling Emotional Situations**
  Travel can be stressful, and some passengers might become anxious or upset, especially if they struggle with certain conditions. Training helps staff stay calm and supportive.

Airlines also include such training for flight attendants, so the same approach extends aboard the plane.

Restrooms and Shower Facilities

Airport restrooms might have special stalls for travelers who use wheelchairs, with wider doors, grab bars, and lower sinks. Some also have automatic door openers. Family restrooms allow a parent to assist a child or a caregiver to help an adult with limited mobility. These rooms offer more privacy and space. Airports in certain regions may provide adult changing tables, especially helpful for travelers with severe disabilities who need to lie down for a change.

Larger airports might have pay-to-use shower facilities or lounges with showers, beneficial for travelers on long flights. These often include accessible shower stalls with bench seats and handrails. Staff can help carry luggage or store it outside the stall if requested.

Visual and Spatial Guiding Features

Beyond braille signs, airports use color-coded paths on floors or overhead signs. They might also place large, easy-to-see symbols. For instance, the arrow for baggage claim can be bright yellow on a dark background. Some airports set up digital monitors at key junctions, showing a map of the terminal and steps to reach each gate. A traveler can tap on the gate number to see a path drawn on the screen. In advanced setups, a traveler's phone can connect to airport Wi-Fi and get step-by-step guidance, possibly with voice instructions.

Addressing Sensory Sensitivities

Loud announcements, bright lights, and crowds can overwhelm some travelers, like those on the autism spectrum or with certain anxiety issues. Airports might create:

- **Low-Sensory Hours or Zones**
  During specific times, lights are dimmed, and announcements are quieter. Or a corner of the terminal might be designated as a calm zone.
- **Noise-Cancelling Pod Seats**
  Some airports experiment with small pods or booths where a traveler can sit in a quieter environment.
- **Optional Staff Alerts**
  A traveler can request staff not to approach them unless necessary, or to speak softly. Clear communication about personal comfort helps staff adapt their approach.

Finding Assistance Before Travel

Travelers who know they need help can often arrange it in advance. When booking a ticket, there might be a section to note mobility or medical needs. After that, the airline or airport can be prepared with wheelchairs, interpreters, or special meal requests. It is wise to contact the airline's special services department a few days before flying, verifying details like:

- **Wheelchair pick-up location**
- **Oxygen device requirements**
- **Seating preferences (e.g., near the restroom)**
- **Permission for service animals or specialized equipment**

Early planning reduces last-minute confusion. If an airport does not know a traveler needs help, they might not have staff ready, causing delays and stress on travel day.

Local and International Accessibility Laws

In many regions, laws protect the rights of travelers with disabilities. For instance:

- **United States**: The Air Carrier Access Act requires airlines to provide certain services. The Americans with Disabilities Act influences airport design.
- **Europe**: The European Union has regulations on passenger rights, covering assistance from airport entrances to planes.
- **Other Countries**: Various laws and guidelines ensure that new terminals have ramps, lifts, tactile surfaces, and accessible restrooms.

Airports must meet building codes that specify how wide ramps must be, how tall counters can be for wheelchair users, and how many accessible restrooms are needed. Inspectors check for compliance, and airports might face fines if they fail to meet standards.

Support During Security Checks

Security screening can be tough for passengers with different needs. For example:

- **Prosthetics or Metal Implants**
  These might trigger alarms. Security officers are trained to do pat-downs or use handheld scanners politely. They should avoid asking the traveler to remove a prosthetic unless absolutely necessary.
- **Wheelchair Users**
  Some are asked to move to a separate area for a pat-down, because they cannot pass through the walk-through scanner easily. Officers often request permission before touching the wheelchair.
- **Medical Devices**
  Devices like insulin pumps or pacemakers could be harmed by certain scanners. Passengers show a doctor's note or declare it, so they receive an alternate screening method.
- **Nonverbal Passengers**
  If someone cannot speak or has difficulty understanding instructions, staff use gestures or step-by-step demonstrations to guide them. They might also keep paper forms or pictures on hand.

Evacuation Planning for All

In emergencies—like a fire in the terminal or an evacuation from the plane—airports must ensure everyone can get out safely:

- **Training Staff**
  They learn how to help someone in a wheelchair down stairs if escalators or elevators shut down. Special evacuation chairs can carry a passenger along steps.
- **Clear Markings**
  Exits have large signs. Some airports place tactile or illuminated floor strips that can guide people who have trouble seeing overhead signs.
- **Announcements**
  If the loudspeaker fails or if travelers are deaf, staff may use flashing lights or approach them directly to explain the situation.
- **Meeting Points**
  Sheltered waiting areas on each floor can hold travelers who cannot use stairs until firefighters arrive with evacuation equipment.

Ongoing Improvements and Innovations

Accessibility is always evolving. Airports keep researching better ideas:

- **Automation**: Touch-screen kiosks that are wheelchair-accessible, with voice guidance for blind travelers.
- **Wearable Tech**: Smart glasses or phone apps that describe the traveler's surroundings.
- **Hidden Disability Initiatives**: More airports adopt special lanyards or pins to help staff identify travelers who might need quiet communication or extra time.
- **Passenger Feedback**: Many airports encourage travelers to share experiences or suggestions, leading to updates in signage, staff training, or layout improvements.
- **Universal Design**: Instead of adding ramps or lifts after building, new airports plan wide hallways, gentle slopes, and well-placed railings from the start.

Air travel becomes smoother for everyone when it is built on the idea that all persons have different needs that can be met in a respectful and practical way.

Concluding Thoughts

Helping people with different needs is not just about following rules. It is about ensuring air travel is welcoming and safe for everyone. From specialized wheelchairs and braille signs to quiet rooms and well-trained staff, airports put effort into removing barriers. Passengers who might be nervous or uncertain due to a disability, a language barrier, or traveling with small kids can find support that eases the process.

This commitment starts with airport design—wider pathways, accessible restrooms, clear signs—and continues with staff prepared to offer a guiding hand or a kind word. Airlines support this, too, by offering early boarding, special diets, or in-flight help. Together, these efforts show that airports value every individual who walks through their doors.

No one wants to feel stranded or helpless in a huge terminal. By planning ahead, speaking up about needs, and using the resources airports provide, travelers can have a more comfortable experience. The airport environment has improved over time and will likely keep adapting as new technologies and ideas appear. In the chapters ahead, we will look at other ways airports try to reduce noise, protect the planet, and handle emergencies. But remembering that travelers come in all forms is a key part of making air travel better for all.

CHAPTER 17: NOISE AND AIRPORTS

Airplanes are powerful machines. Their engines make a strong roar when they take off, climb, and land. While this sound might be exciting or interesting for people who enjoy watching planes, it can also be a problem for those who live or work near an airport. The noise can disturb sleep, affect comfort, and make everyday life harder. In this chapter, we will look at why airports can be noisy, how noise is measured, and the many ways people try to reduce or control it. We will see that airport noise is a challenge that involves careful planning and cooperation between airlines, airport managers, local communities, and government agencies.

Why Airports Are Noisy

1. **Engine Power**
   Airplane engines burn fuel to create thrust, which pushes the plane forward. Large jets require huge amounts of thrust to lift off the ground. This combustion process can be extremely loud. A jet engine sucks in air, compresses it, mixes it with fuel, and then ignites the mixture. The hot gases rush out the back at high speed, creating noise. Even smaller turboprop planes make a noticeable buzz, though less than the roar of large jets.

2. **Aerodynamics**
   As planes move through the air, they create wind-like sounds around wings and flaps. This effect is quieter than engine noise but still contributes. During descent, when flaps and landing gear are extended, the airflow around these parts can produce additional sound.
3. **Reverse Thrust**
   After a plane lands, some jets use reverse thrust to slow down. This means the engine's output is briefly redirected to push air forward instead of backward. It can cause a loud burst of sound, especially near the runway ends.
4. **Ground Operations**
   Noise at airports is not just from takeoffs and landings. Ground vehicles, baggage carts, and auxiliary power units (small engines attached to planes on the ground) also add to the noise. However, these are typically quieter than a jet at full thrust.

Airports can have many flights each day, which repeats these noises over and over. The volume depends on factors like the number of runways, the types of planes, and how close houses or buildings are to the flight paths.

How We Measure and Describe Noise

People often think of loudness in decibels (dB). A decibel is a unit used to measure sound intensity. The higher the number, the louder the sound. For example, normal conversation might be around 60 dB, a busy street about 70–80 dB, and a jet takeoff could exceed 100 dB if you are very close. Because the human ear perceives sound in a complex way, and because we do not hear all frequencies equally, specialists often use "A-weighted decibels" (dBA) to better match how our ears work.

Additionally, noise at airports is not just measured at one single moment. Instead, there are measures like the "Day-Night Average Sound Level" (DNL), which gives a combined view of the noise over 24 hours, with extra weighting for nighttime noise. If planes fly late at night, that can disturb sleep, so those hours count more in noise studies. Some places use an Lden measure (day-evening-night) that adds extra weight for evening and night hours. These averages help planners and government agencies understand the total noise impact on communities around the airport.

Noise modeling is also used. Experts create virtual maps of airplane flight paths, typical aircraft types, and daily schedules. They combine this information with known noise levels for different engines and flight phases. Then they produce "noise contours" on a map, drawing lines around areas that experience certain levels of average noise. People living inside the contour with, for example, 65 dBA DNL might be strongly affected by airport noise, while those outside the contour might hear planes but not as loudly.

The Effects of Noise on People

Excessive noise can cause problems for people living near busy airports:

1. **Sleep Disruption**
   Late-night or early-morning flights can wake people up or keep them from resting. Even if someone does not fully wake, noise can cause shallow sleep or frequent tossing and turning. Consistent disruption can affect mood and health over time.
2. **Communication Difficulties**
   It can be hard to talk or listen when a plane passes overhead. At schools near an airport, teachers might pause lessons until the plane noise fades. This interrupts the flow of learning and can be frustrating for everyone.
3. **Stress and Annoyance**
   Constant noise, especially when unpredictable, raises stress levels and irritates many. People might feel helpless if they have no power to stop or reduce the noise. This can lead to anger toward the airport or local officials.
4. **Health Concerns**
   Some studies suggest that long-term exposure to high levels of noise may contribute to cardiovascular issues like high blood pressure. Not everyone agrees on how strong this effect is, but it is an ongoing area of research.

Because of these impacts, airports often work with local leaders to find methods of noise control or at least limit noise during nighttime hours.

Noise Abatement and Flight Paths

Airlines and airports use noise abatement procedures to reduce the sound that reaches neighborhoods. These procedures might include:

1. **Preferred Runways**
   If the wind allows, controllers select the runway that directs planes away from dense residential areas. For instance, some airports have one runway pointing out over farmland or water, and they encourage using that one when possible.
2. **Steep Climb Out**
   After takeoff, pilots might climb more steeply than usual to gain altitude quickly, thereby reducing noise for people living near the runway. However, each plane has limits on how steep it can climb safely without performance issues.
3. **Reduced Power Settings**
   Some airlines reduce engine power earlier once they are at a safe altitude. This lowers noise, but the pilot and airline must balance it with fuel efficiency and safety requirements.
4. **Continuous Descent Approaches (CDA)**
   Rather than the plane stepping down in stages (leveling off multiple times), a continuous descent approach lets it glide smoothly downward from cruise altitude to runway. This can cut engine noise and reduce the need for throttle changes, which can be noisy.
5. **Routing Over Less Populated Areas**
   When planning flight paths, controllers try to send planes over industrial zones, highways, or bodies of water rather than thickly populated neighborhoods. This is not always possible, but where it is, it helps limit the number of people affected.

These measures aim to keep noise footprints as small as possible while still maintaining safe flight operations.

Curfews and Nighttime Restrictions

Because nighttime noise disrupts sleep more severely, many airports have special rules for late or very early hours:

1. **Full Night Curfew**
   Some airports ban scheduled takeoffs and landings during certain hours, for example from 11:00 p.m. to 6:00 a.m. This policy ensures residents can sleep without being startled by jet engines.
2. **Partial Curfew**
   In some cases, only certain aircraft types are restricted at night. Older,

noisier jets might be banned, while newer, quieter planes can still operate. Or cargo flights might have stricter rules.

3. **Noise Quotas**
   A few airports allow a limited number of "night noise units" per season. Each plane type has a rating. Airlines must plan so they do not exceed that total rating. This encourages them to use quieter jets if they must fly at night.

Curfews can be controversial because they limit the airport's operational hours, affecting airline schedules and cargo business. But many communities see them as necessary to preserve quality of life. In places without a curfew, residents sometimes protest if flights continue into the late night or start very early.

Quiet Engine Designs and Technology

The aviation industry tries to make quieter planes. Over the decades, jet engines have changed drastically:

- **High Bypass Ratio Engines**
  Modern engines push a lot of air around the core instead of through it. This design lowers the speed of the exhaust flow, reducing noise compared to older turbojets.
- **Acoustic Liners**
  Engine manufacturers place sound-absorbing materials inside the engine casing to dampen noise. You might see the chevrons (serrated edges) on some engine nozzles, which help mix the exhaust with surrounding air more smoothly, lowering the roar.
- **Better Aerodynamics**
  Wing designs, winglets, and flaps can reduce turbulence and whistling noises. Computer simulations help identify and minimize these sources of sound.
- **Procedures to Limit Reverse Thrust**
  If the runway is long enough, pilots can rely more on brakes and less on reverse thrust after landing. This approach lowers the sudden roar that can happen right after touchdown.

These upgrades have helped modern jets become far quieter than ones from decades ago. However, even improved designs still create noticeable noise at takeoff, so additional measures remain necessary.

Noise Insulation for Homes

Some airports sponsor insulation programs, paying for or contributing to noise-reducing modifications in homes near flight paths. These might include:

1. **Upgraded Windows**
   Installing double- or triple-pane windows can greatly reduce outside noise. Some have special laminated glass that blocks sound frequencies typical of jet engines.
2. **Improved Doors**
   Solid, well-sealed doors keep out noise better than hollow or thin ones. Weather stripping can close gaps around the edges.
3. **Roof and Wall Insulation**
   Adding insulation or thicker layers in walls and roofs can dampen sound. This helps residents sleep better and enjoy quieter indoor spaces.
4. **Air Conditioning**
   If people keep windows closed to block noise, they need a way to cool the home. Some insulation programs may help fund or install central air systems so they do not have to open windows in hot weather.

To qualify, homeowners often must live within certain noise contours, such as 65 dBA DNL or higher. By funding such programs, airports acknowledge the impact on neighbors and try to help them cope.

Communication with Communities

An airport cannot operate successfully if it clashes with the local community. Many airports:

- **Hold Public Meetings**
  They invite neighbors, local businesses, and officials to discuss noise issues and possible solutions. This helps both sides understand each other's concerns.
- **Noise Complaint Systems**
  Airports set up hotlines or web forms where residents can report loud events or unusual flight paths. Staff review these complaints to see if something was out of the ordinary or if a plane flew off the standard route.

- **Noise Management Committees**
  Some airports have committees with representatives from the airport, airlines, local authorities, and citizen groups. They meet regularly to review noise levels, discuss complaints, and propose improvements.
- **Transparent Noise Monitoring**
  Stations around the airport measure actual noise day and night. The airport publishes these results, showing whether certain neighborhoods exceed recommended levels. When people see data openly, it builds trust.

These efforts do not erase noise entirely, but they help involve the public in decision-making. Residents might better accept some noise if they know the airport is taking real steps to minimize it.

Restricting Noisy Aircraft (Chapter Stages)

Some older jets create noise much worse than modern planes. Governments and airports sometimes ban or strictly limit these:

- **Chapter 2, 3, 4, and 14 Aircraft**
  The International Civil Aviation Organization (ICAO) sets noise standards in "chapters." Chapter 2 aircraft were older, noisier planes mostly phased out in many places. Chapter 3 brought stricter limits, and Chapter 4 was even quieter. More recently, Chapter 14 sets an even higher standard for new aircraft designs. Airlines retiring older planes or upgrading to meet new chapters helps reduce noise over time.
- **Penalty Fees**
  Airports may charge extra fees if an airline lands with a plane above a certain noise level. This pricing encourages carriers to use quieter models or schedule flights for daytime if they must bring in a louder plane.
- **Local Rules**
  Some airports say, "No Stage 2 or Chapter 2 jets can operate here." Or they confine them to limited hours. The goal is to push airlines away from older, louder engines.

As a result, fleets in many countries now consist mostly of Chapter 3 or 4 planes, which are quieter and less disruptive.

Building Runways Farther from Homes

When planners design or expand an airport, they prefer to keep flight paths away from dense neighborhoods. However, this is not always possible if the airport is surrounded by urban areas. In some places:

- **New Runways**
  If a runway is added, the airport might buy land around it or set "land use rules" to prevent new houses from being built close by. This approach helps create a buffer zone.
- **Moving Entire Airports**
  Rarely, a city decides to build a new airport far from populated zones and close or repurpose the old one. This is very costly and time-consuming but can solve noise problems near the old airport. It can also spark complaints from people living near the new site.
- **Land Use Planning**
  Local zoning laws can forbid schools, hospitals, or dense housing in high-noise areas. Instead, the land might be used for warehouses, factories, or open spaces. This practice reduces the number of people affected by flight noise.

Despite careful planning, airports sometimes outgrow their surroundings. Over decades, a once-remote site can become ringed by development, leading to noise disputes.

Double Approaches, Alternating Runways

Some large airports have multiple runways. To distribute noise more fairly, they might rotate which runways are used:

- **Alternating Approaches**
  Certain days or hours use one runway's approach path, then switch to another. This rotation means one neighborhood does not get every single arrival. Each area might get a break on certain days.
- **Preferential Runway Use**
  If the wind direction is calm or light, the tower chooses runways that direct traffic away from dense populations. This strategy is not always possible if the wind picks up from a certain direction.

- **Arrival and Departure Patterns**
  Sometimes departures always go off one runway, arrivals on another, so that no single area has both. This does not fix noise but might reduce total annoyance for certain neighborhoods.

The success of these strategies depends on many factors: runway layout, wind, and flight volume. At busy airports with 24-hour operations, runway rotation can be complicated, but it helps share the noise burden.

Helicopter and Small Plane Noise

Not all airport noise comes from commercial jets. Helicopters and small propeller planes can also create disturbance, especially if they hover or do repeated practice landings:

- **Helicopter Routes**
  Helicopters might follow designated corridors away from homes. This can be tricky in cities where hospitals use helipads. Police or news helicopters might circle overhead, increasing noise for certain spots.
- **Flight Training**
  Student pilots practicing touch-and-go landings can repeat the circuit many times, generating repeated buzz in the same area. Some airports set specific hours or direct training flights to less residential spots.
- **Altitude Rules**
  Sometimes small planes must maintain a higher altitude over populated zones, reducing the loudness below. If they need to descend, they try to do so over less sensitive areas.

Local flight clubs or training schools often meet with community leaders to address concerns about droning propellers or repeated overflights.

Noise Barriers and Landscaping

Physical structures can help a little, though they are not a perfect solution:

- **Earth Berms**
  Some airports build tall earthen mounds near runways or taxiways. These mounds act like walls, absorbing some engine noise. However, large jets

are so high when taking off that much of the sound travels above the berm.

- **Noise Walls**
  Tall barriers made of special materials can reduce ground-level noise from ground vehicles or idle jets, but they do not block noise from planes at altitude. These walls may help for maintenance or taxi areas where engines run at lower speeds.
- **Trees and Green Belts**
  Lines of trees have a small effect on reducing noise, but they are more useful visually or for capturing dust. They do not significantly block the loud roar of a departing jet. Still, they can provide some aesthetic relief and help with wind or glare.

Because planes fly high, none of these barriers solve the main cause of overhead noise. Yet they can lessen smaller ground noise or engine testing noise.

Engine Run-Up and Maintenance Noise

Aircraft engines sometimes need testing or "run-ups" after repairs. If this is done near houses, it can be very disturbing:

- **Designated Run-Up Areas**
  Airports often have special enclosures or areas away from the main terminal and neighborhoods. These areas might have tall barriers to contain noise. Technicians can secure the plane in place and power up the engines to test them without exposing everyone nearby to the full blast.
- **Restricted Times**
  Maintenance run-ups may be banned at night or only allowed at certain hours. If an urgent repair needs a test late at night, the airline might request special permission, but it is rare.
- **Recording and Monitoring**
  If someone complains about engine testing noise, the airport checks logs to see when and where a run-up happened. If it was outside allowed hours, the airline or maintenance team could face a penalty.

These rules aim to balance the need for safe aircraft maintenance with the need for quieter surroundings.

Technology and Quieter Approaches

Air navigation service providers are testing new systems:

- **Required Navigation Performance (RNP)**
  With more precise satellite navigation, planes can fly narrower paths. This means they can avoid certain neighborhoods if done carefully. However, it might concentrate flights over fewer areas, which can be good or bad depending on local preferences.
- **Glide Slope Adjustments**
  Some airports raise the glide path slightly, so planes approach at a steeper angle. A half-degree difference might keep them higher above residential zones, reducing noise on the ground.
- **Noise Monitoring in Real Time**
  Networks of microphones around the airport record noise levels and link them to specific flights. If a pilot used higher thrust than normal, or strayed off the route, the system flags it. Airlines might be warned or fined if they repeatedly fail to follow noise abatement procedures.

Balancing Growth and Community Needs

Air travel is important for trade, tourism, and economic development. Airports create jobs and link regions. However, as an airport grows busier, noise issues can escalate. Balancing these factors is complicated:

- **Economic Arguments**
  Airports say growth benefits everyone: more flights, more business, more tourism, and cheaper travel. They highlight job creation from airlines, ground staff, shops, and cargo operations.
- **Community Concerns**
  Neighbors point to sleepless nights, stress, and lower property values. They argue that unchecked expansion makes living near the airport unbearable.
- **Compromises**
  Often, expansions proceed with noise mitigation. The airport might build a new runway but pay for insulation or even buy out homes in the highest noise zones. They might implement stricter curfews or approach paths. Public hearings and environmental impact statements are part of this process.

In many cases, legal battles or protests occur if communities feel they are not heard. Over time, airports and governments try to reach solutions that allow growth without overwhelming neighborhoods.

Research and Future Outlook

Experts keep looking for ways to lower noise:

- **Quieter Supersonic Jets?**
  Research teams are designing supersonic planes with shapes that reduce the sonic boom. If such planes come back into regular service, their booms must be minimized to avoid mass disturbance.
- **Engine Developments**
  Engine companies test "open-rotor" designs or advanced fans that might cut noise further. Electric or hybrid planes might reduce engine roar at certain phases, though large electric jets are still far off.
- **Sound Mapping and AI**
  Using big data, computers can predict noise footprints more accurately. AI might suggest real-time route tweaks to minimize total noise for communities based on weather, time of day, or local conditions.
- **Urban Air Mobility**
  Smaller electric vertical-takeoff vehicles (like air taxis) are being developed. If they become common, city skies might get busier. Regulators must set noise limits or routes to avoid irritating city residents. The promise is that electric motors are quieter than helicopter engines, but people worry about the cumulative effect of many such craft.

Given these possibilities, noise control remains a key topic for future airports. As technology improves, the goal is to find solutions that let planes fly with less disturbance.

Airports Working with Airlines

Airlines are on the front lines of noise reduction because they choose aircraft types and set flight schedules. Airports might:

- **Give Discounts for Quieter Jets**
  Landing fees can be lower if the plane is in a quieter category. This encourages airlines to upgrade or keep the quietest jets on that route.

- **Coordinate Timetables**
  If late-night flights are unavoidable, the airport might push airlines to use modern planes with advanced noise suppression. They might also cluster flights so residents have periods of silence rather than a constant stream.
- **Publish Performance Rankings**
  Some airports publicly rank airlines on noise performance, praising those with fewer complaints or lower decibel readings. This can create positive peer pressure among airlines to adopt quieter procedures.
- **Airline Training**
  Pilots learn noise abatement takeoff and landing steps. Airlines might require flight crews to reduce thrust carefully or follow continuous descent. Coordinating with air traffic control is essential, so the plane can fly these procedures safely.

All parties must talk openly, because while an airline might prefer maximum efficiency (burning less fuel by certain flight paths), the airport may push for a quieter route that could use a bit more fuel. Finding a middle ground is an ongoing task.

Noise Complaints and Solutions

People's tolerance for noise varies. One neighbor may ignore jets overhead, while another might be highly annoyed by any nighttime flight. Airport managers handle countless noise complaints, some repeated by the same individual:

- **Complaint Analysis**
  They track how many complaints come from each neighborhood. A sudden spike might mean a new route has started or more night flights occurred. Reviewing flight data can confirm if something changed.
- **Open House Events**
  Airports might invite neighbors to see control towers or meet airline staff. When residents understand how safety, weather, and scheduling affect flight paths, they might be more patient. Also, seeing new technology for quieter planes can reassure them improvements are happening.
- **Legal Challenges**
  In extreme cases, residents sue the airport or local authorities for noise pollution. Courts might order stricter regulations or pay compensation. Usually, though, airports try to solve issues before it reaches that stage.

- **Long-Term Planning**
  If an airport foresees growth, it might buy land in advance or set noise limits early to avoid bigger problems later. Proactive measures can reduce future arguments and lawsuits.

Concluding Thoughts

Noise is one of the biggest side effects of having an airport in or near a community. Planes bring many benefits—fast travel, cargo delivery, tourism—but the roar of engines can disrupt daily life. Over the years, technology and rules have cut noise significantly. Modern jets are much quieter than older ones, and many airports apply curfews, flight path management, and building insulation to lessen the disturbance. But no solution eliminates noise entirely. Balancing growth with peace and quiet is an ongoing process.

Communities keep pushing for less noise, and airports keep seeking ways to operate more quietly. Government regulations, advanced aircraft design, and new procedures help. Sometimes, these changes are slow or expensive. Yet, over time, the continuous push from neighbors, local governments, and global aviation standards leads to quieter skies. It is a partnership—airports, airlines, and the public working together to ensure that flying remains convenient while nearby families can rest more easily. In the next chapter, we will examine how airports care for the environment beyond noise, seeking cleaner operations for land, air, and water.

CHAPTER 18: WAYS TO BE KINDER TO THE EARTH

Airports and airplanes help people move quickly and ship goods around the world. Yet this activity can affect the planet. From engine exhaust to energy use, airports and airlines face challenges in being friendlier to the environment. Many have taken steps to limit harmful impacts, such as reducing carbon emissions, handling waste responsibly, and protecting local wildlife. In this chapter, we will look at what airports do to become more earth-friendly. We will explore how changes in design, technology, and daily operations can make flying a cleaner choice for everyone.

The Main Environmental Concerns

1. **Air Pollution**
   Airplanes burn fuel, releasing gases into the sky. On the ground, ground vehicles and support systems also create emissions. Key concerns include carbon dioxide (CO_2), which contributes to global warming, and nitrogen oxides (NOx), which affect air quality near the airport.
2. **Carbon Footprint**
   The carbon footprint is the total amount of greenhouse gases produced by an activity—here, it is the sum of all emissions from planes, vehicles, electricity use, heating, etc. Aviation's global share of CO_2 is smaller than some industries, but it is expected to rise as air travel grows.
3. **Waste and Water Usage**
   Airports handle large amounts of trash from passengers, restaurants, and shops. They also use water for cooling, cleaning, and landscaping. Poor management can strain local resources or pollute water bodies.
4. **Climate Change Effects**
   As the planet warms, airports near coasts may face rising sea levels. Hotter temperatures can affect airplane performance. Storms might grow stronger. So, airports must adapt to these changes in addition to reducing their own impact.

These concerns drive airports to create strategies that preserve the environment while serving travelers.

Modern and Efficient Buildings

Airports often have huge terminals, parking structures, and hangars. Building and operating them uses plenty of energy. To lower the environmental impact:

1. **Green Building Standards**
   Some airports follow certifications like LEED (Leadership in Energy and Environmental Design) or BREEAM (in some countries). These require using eco-friendly materials, efficient lighting, and proper insulation.
2. **Natural Lighting**
   Large windows and skylights can reduce the need for artificial lights during the day. Clever terminal designs let sunlight brighten waiting areas, which can also help with passenger well-being.
3. **Better Insulation and Cooling**
   Keeping a terminal at a comfortable temperature can be energy-heavy. By using high-quality insulation, double-pane windows, and efficient air conditioning, airports waste less energy. Some even use "green roofs" covered with plants that help regulate building temperature.
4. **Automatic Systems**
   Motion sensors or timers can turn off lights and escalators in areas not in use, such as late-night hours in empty hallways. Smart climate controls adjust cooling or heating based on the number of passengers inside.
5. **Solar Panels**
   Some airports install solar farms on unused land or rooftops. This clean energy can power parts of the terminal or feed into the local grid. A well-placed solar array might offset a significant portion of the airport's electricity demand.

Over time, these measures reduce costs and carbon emissions, showing that being kinder to the earth can also make financial sense.

Cutting Carbon Emissions from Flights

While the airport terminal itself uses energy, the biggest chunk of aviation emissions comes from planes in the sky. Airports cannot fully control that, but they do take steps:

1. **Improved Taxi and Ground Handling**
   Planes sometimes idle engines for long stretches while taxiing or waiting.

Some airports supply electric ground power so that planes can switch off their main engines when parked, using a cleaner energy source. This cuts fuel burn and exhaust on the ramp.

2. **Shorter Taxi Routes**

   By designing taxiways that minimize time on the ground, planes can roll straight to the runway without lots of waiting. The less time planes spend taxiing with engines running, the less fuel they waste.

3. **Continuous Descent Operations**

   If air traffic control allows planes to glide down from cruise altitude in a smooth path, they use less engine thrust. This saves fuel and reduces emissions. The same is true for modern climb procedures that minimize time at lower, denser altitudes.

4. **Green Fuel Initiatives**

   Some airports partner with airlines to offer sustainable aviation fuels (SAF), made from used cooking oil or other organic sources. SAF can cut the net carbon output compared to standard jet fuel. Although it is still more expensive and not yet widely available, each step helps.

5. **Encouraging Newer Planes**

   Airports might give fee reductions or priority slots to airlines using newer, more efficient aircraft. For example, a Boeing 787 or Airbus A350 has lower emissions than older planes. This approach nudges airlines to invest in eco-friendly fleets.

Cleaner Ground Vehicles

Anyone who looks out from the terminal sees baggage carts, fuel trucks, catering vehicles, and more. They usually run on diesel or gasoline, adding to pollution. To clean this up:

1. **Electric Carts and Tugs**

   Some airports replace old baggage tractors with electric ones. They can be charged at stations near the gates. This swap reduces fumes and noise. Maintenance can also be simpler because electric motors have fewer moving parts.

2. **Alternative Fuels**

   Vehicles that run on compressed natural gas (CNG), biodiesel, or hydrogen are tested at some airports. This helps cut harmful emissions and lower carbon footprints.

3. **Fuel-Saving Routines**
   Drivers are trained to switch off engines if they are idling for more than a short time. Routes around the ramp can be streamlined to avoid unnecessary driving.
4. **Shared Services**
   Multiple airlines can share ground vehicles to avoid having too many separate fleets. If well-coordinated, this saves resources and space on the tarmac.

As technology improves, more airports are pushing toward a fully electric fleet, making ground operations much cleaner.

Water Conservation and Pollution Control

Airports use water for many tasks—cleaning planes, washing vehicles, drinking water for passengers, watering landscaping, and cooling systems in large buildings. To conserve water:

- **Recycling and Reusing**
  Airports install systems that recycle water from sinks or rainwater to use for flushing toilets or irrigation. Some have advanced treatment plants to clean used water so it can be reused in non-drinking ways.
- **Low-Flow Fixtures**
  Restrooms may have faucets with sensors or low-flow toilets that cut down water waste. Because of the huge number of travelers, saving even a little per person adds up.
- **De-Icing Fluids**
  In snowy climates, planes require de-icing fluid. That fluid can run off into drains, affecting local waterways. Modern airports collect and recycle this fluid. They have special pads where planes are sprayed, and the leftover flows into a treatment system instead of the environment.
- **Fuel and Chemical Spills**
  Handling large volumes of jet fuel creates a risk of spills. Airports have spill response teams and containment measures. If a leak happens, they quickly block it, use absorbents, and dispose of waste properly to prevent groundwater or river contamination.

Waste Management and Recycling

With restaurants, shops, and tens of thousands of passengers daily, airports produce lots of trash. Items range from paper cups to food scraps and plastic packaging. Some steps to reduce waste:

1. **Recycling Bins**
   Strategically placed bins encourage travelers to sort recyclables like paper, bottles, and cans. Signs or color coding helps visitors know where to place items.
2. **Composting**
   Food waste from restaurants can be collected for compost instead of going to a landfill. In some airports, staff separate organic leftovers to send to a compost facility or an anaerobic digester (which produces biogas).
3. **Encouraging Reusable Materials**
   Cafes might offer discounts for travelers who bring their own coffee cups. Stores can reduce plastic bag use or switch to paper or biodegradable options.
4. **Donating Unused Items**
   Some shops or lounges might have leftover goods—like packaged sandwiches close to expiry—that can be donated to local shelters if local laws allow. This helps reduce food waste and supports communities.
5. **Construction Debris**
   Renovations or expansions produce concrete, metal, and wood scraps. Airports aim to recycle or reuse these instead of dumping them. Responsible contractors must follow green guidelines for handling construction materials.

By sorting and handling waste carefully, airports can cut down on landfill use and reduce pollution.

Preserving Local Ecosystems

An airport might occupy large sections of land that once belonged to nature. To protect wildlife and habitats:

- **Wildlife Management**
  Airports keep animals away from runways for safety reasons. However,

they also create buffer zones with grass or wetlands that can be a home for smaller species. They might carefully handle these zones to keep them from attracting large flocks of birds that could collide with planes.

- **Protected Areas**
  If building a runway near wetlands or forests, the airport may set up conservation programs. They might restore another area to offset the loss of habitat, or create special corridors for animals to move safely around the airport perimeter.
- **Tree Planting**
  Some airports replant trees or establish green spaces around car parks or approach roads. Trees help absorb carbon dioxide and provide shade, though they must be carefully placed so they do not attract large birds near flight paths.
- **Controlling Light Pollution**
  Runway and terminal lights can confuse nocturnal animals or migrating birds. Designers try to direct light downward, minimize unnecessary glare, and use colors that limit disruption to wildlife. Less glare also helps reduce wasted energy.

Noise Control Helps the Planet, Too

Earlier, we focused on noise for community health. But noise control steps can also aid the environment. For instance:

- **Steeper Climbs**
  A steep climb out means the plane gains altitude quickly, which can use extra engine power short-term, but it might let it reach more efficient cruise settings sooner. The effect on total emissions varies. However, if properly designed, noise abatement procedures can still be part of more efficient flight paths.
- **Curfews**
  Having fewer flights at night might mean less continuous operation of ground services. Some ground equipment can be turned off or scheduled to power down at night, lowering energy use.
- **Modern Jets**
  Planes that are quieter tend to be more fuel-efficient, because advanced engine technology and aerodynamics typically reduce both fuel burn and noise. So upgrading to quieter planes often means greener planes overall.

Noise programs can go hand in hand with broader sustainability goals. The same technology or planning that reduces sound often boosts fuel efficiency.

Public Transport Access to Airports

Many people drive cars to reach the airport, adding traffic, pollution, and the need for large parking areas. Encouraging public transport can cut emissions:

1. **Train and Metro Lines**
   Some airports connect directly to city rail systems. Passengers can ride trains from downtown straight to the terminal, avoiding car travel. This saves fuel and reduces road congestion.
2. **Buses and Shuttles**
   Airports might run frequent shuttle buses from main transport hubs. Some use clean-energy buses, like electric or natural gas. If these buses run reliably and affordably, more travelers use them.
3. **Bike Lanes and Pedestrian Paths**
   Though not common for large airports, some smaller or regional airports create safe bike paths or sidewalks. Airport workers might bike if they live nearby. Even if passengers rarely bike to catch flights, staff might do so daily, cutting some commuter emissions.
4. **Parking Policies**
   Higher parking fees can nudge travelers toward other modes of transport. On the other hand, cheap, convenient parking encourages driving. Balancing these fees is part of the airport's strategy to reduce car usage.

By making it easy and pleasant to reach the airport without a car, airports help reduce their overall carbon footprint.

Green Energy and District Heating

Beyond solar panels, airports can tap various energy sources:

- **Wind Turbines**
  In breezy regions with enough space, an airport might install wind turbines. However, tall turbines near runways require careful placement to avoid hazards for planes.
- **Geothermal Systems**
  Some airports use geothermal wells for heating and cooling. Fluid is

circulated underground to pick up or release heat, providing a steady temperature resource.
- **District Heating and Cooling**
  Large airport campuses might have a central plant that generates steam or hot water for multiple buildings. Using combined heat and power (CHP) systems, they can produce electricity and use waste heat to warm terminals, increasing overall efficiency.
- **Energy Storage**
  Batteries can store extra solar or wind power during off-peak hours, then release it when needed. This smooths out fluctuations and helps the airport rely less on the main grid.

Each site picks the best mix based on climate, land availability, and local regulations.

Reducing Single-Use Plastics

Public attention has grown around plastic waste. Airports can address this by:

- **Water Fountains**
  Installing bottle refill stations encourages travelers to bring reusable bottles. Some airports ban the sale of single-use plastic bottles, replacing them with biodegradable containers or aluminum cans.
- **Restaurant Rules**
  Cafés and eateries might stop using plastic straws, or they might switch to paper or biodegradable ones. Take-away utensils can be made of wooden or compostable materials.
- **Retail Shops**
  Airport stores can use paper or cloth bags instead of plastic. Some airports do not hand out bags by default, asking if the customer truly needs one.

Though these changes seem small compared to fuel emissions, it still helps reduce overall waste and teaches travelers to adopt greener habits.

Green Spaces and Passenger Comfort

Some newer terminals feature indoor gardens, living walls, or even small outdoor courtyards. These are not just for looks:

- **Cleaner Air**
  Plants can help filter indoor air, although large ventilation systems do most of the work. Still, greenery adds oxygen and a sense of calm in a busy space.
- **Temperature Control**
  Properly designed indoor vegetation can help regulate humidity. Also, natural shading from trees near windows can reduce cooling needs.
- **Well-Being**
  Studies show plants can help reduce stress. An airport with green areas might help travelers relax, especially during long waits. The environment is more pleasant and less sterile.

Some airports have entire nature-themed zones, with waterfalls, koi ponds, or butterfly gardens. Though it takes maintenance and water, the net effect can be an improved passenger experience and a reminder that we share our spaces with living things.

Carbon Offsets and Airport Programs

Some airports offer carbon offset programs for flights or even for general airport operations:

- **Offset Projects**
  Money from offsets funds tree planting, wind farms, or other greenhouse gas-cutting projects. Passengers can opt to pay a small fee when buying tickets to offset the CO2 from their flight.
- **Airport Neutrality**
  A few airports aim to be "carbon neutral," at least for their ground operations. They calculate all emissions from heating, vehicles, and electricity, reduce where possible, and buy offsets for what remains. This does not cover the airplanes in the sky, but it is a start for the ground-side footprint.
- **Skepticism and Verification**
  Some people question whether offsets truly solve the root problem. That is why recognized certification schemes (like Gold Standard or Verified Carbon Standard) exist to ensure offset projects are real and helpful. Airports also must keep working on direct emission cuts, not just offsets.

Encouraging Airlines to Use Sustainable Fuels

Sustainable Aviation Fuel (SAF) is a hot topic. Some airports:

1. **Provide Infrastructure**
   SAF might need different storage or blending facilities. If the airport invests in that, airlines can more easily fuel up with a certain percentage of SAF.
2. **Mandates or Incentives**
   A region or airport authority might require a small fraction of the fuel to be from renewable sources. Or they might give cost breaks for airlines that choose SAF. This can spur more widespread adoption.
3. **Awareness Campaigns**
   Informing passengers about which flights use SAF can build demand. People who care about the environment might prefer an airline that uses some green fuel, even if it costs a bit more.

While SAF alone will not solve everything, it can reduce life-cycle CO_2 emissions. The main challenge is cost and availability, but each year progress is made.

Handling Spills and Hazardous Materials

Besides fuel, airports deal with chemicals (de-icers, solvents, cleaning agents). They must store these safely and have quick cleanup plans:

- **Spill Kits**
  Absorbent materials, booms, and protective suits are on hand. If a tanker leaks, ground staff respond fast to stop it spreading into soil or water systems.
- **Hazardous Waste Disposal**
  Old batteries, electronics, or used chemical containers should be disposed of in line with environmental rules. The airport might partner with certified waste handlers to ensure safe disposal.
- **Monitoring Wells**
  Some airports set up wells around the property to test groundwater regularly. If contamination appears, they investigate the source. Quick action can prevent larger damage.

This careful approach keeps toxins away from local ecosystems and drinking water.

Education for Staff and Passengers

A green airport depends on people's actions:

- **Staff Training**
  Everyone from maintenance crews to restaurant workers learns about recycling, energy saving, spill procedures, and water conservation. They might get regular updates on new guidelines or best practices.
- **Passenger Awareness**
  Signs and announcements remind travelers about water bottle refill stations, recycling bins, or how to dispose of liquids. Some airports show real-time energy usage on big screens to encourage a shared sense of responsibility.
- **Green Guidelines for Tenants**
  Shops and airlines renting space in the airport must follow environment-friendly policies, like turning off lights when closed or using energy-efficient appliances. Restaurants might sign a contract to recycle and reduce food waste.

A culture of sustainability grows when everyone sees it as part of daily routine.

Dealing with Climate Change Effects

No matter how green they try to be, airports also have to face the changing climate:

1. **Extreme Weather Readiness**
   More heat waves can warp runways, more storms might flood terminals, stronger winds can disrupt flights. Airports reinforce drainage systems, upgrade runway materials, and expand backup power supplies.
2. **Sea-Level Rise**
   Coastal airports risk flooding in the future. Some are already building sea walls or planning to move key systems to higher ground. They also consider building new runways farther inland if possible.
3. **Heat Limits on Aircraft**
   If it gets too hot, planes need more runway to take off. Some airports

schedule flights at cooler times or lengthen runways. They also watch for peak temperature periods that might disrupt regular schedules.

By planning now, airports aim to keep operating smoothly despite unpredictable future conditions. This resilience is part of being kind to the earth: understanding that we must adapt to changes we cannot fully stop.

Partnerships and Global Efforts

Airports often join coalitions or networks to share eco-friendly ideas. Examples include:

- **Airport Carbon Accreditation**
  This program, supported by airports worldwide, recognizes achievements in cutting carbon. Airports advance through levels: Mapping, Reduction, Optimization, and finally, Neutrality, each with stricter targets.
- **Collaborating with Air Traffic Control**
  Procedures like "Collaborative Decision Making" let airlines, the tower, and ground crews coordinate to reduce unnecessary taxi time or holding patterns, saving fuel.
- **ICAO's Environmental Goals**
  The International Civil Aviation Organization sets global goals for reducing emissions, managing noise, and improving sustainability. Although each country sets its own specific rules, these international guidelines steer overall direction.
- **Regional Workshops**
  Airports in a region might hold workshops on green technology, stormwater handling, or new building methods. By learning from each other's successes or mistakes, they improve faster.

These partnerships underscore that environmental issues cross borders. Everyone benefits from cleaner skies and healthier ecosystems.

The Role of Passengers

Travelers themselves can make greener choices:

- **Packing Light**
  A lighter plane uses less fuel. If many people cut down baggage weight, it adds up.
- **Refilling Bottles**
  Bringing a reusable water bottle avoids buying plastic ones.
- **Proper Recycling**
  Sorting trash properly in the terminal helps reduce waste.
- **Choosing Airlines That Show Green Initiatives**
  If enough people prefer carriers investing in fuel-efficient planes or SAF, that encourages the entire industry to go greener.
- **Considering Alternatives**
  If a short flight can be replaced by a train or bus, that might reduce carbon footprint. Of course, not everyone can do this, especially for long international routes.

While airports and airlines hold big responsibilities, passenger actions also shape the future of green air travel.

CHAPTER 19: HANDLING EMERGENCIES

Airports are places where huge numbers of people come and go each day. They welcome airplanes of all sizes, carry valuable cargo, and connect countries around the globe. Because of these busy operations, there is always a possibility that something unexpected could happen. Airports must be prepared to deal with all sorts of emergencies. In this chapter, we will see what steps airports take to handle problems quickly and safely. We will explore everything from airplane incidents and medical needs to natural disasters. You will learn how different airport teams work together to protect travelers, staff, and the surrounding community.

Why Preparedness Is Crucial

An emergency can occur at any time in an airport setting:

- **An airplane might have a mechanical problem and make an emergency landing.**
- **Bad weather, like a hurricane or major snowfall, could force the airport to shut down.**
- **A traveler might get sick or have a serious medical condition.**
- **A fire could break out in the terminal or in an airplane's cargo hold.**
- **Dangerous goods might leak or catch fire.**

Because airports usually run all day and night, staff must be ready. They cannot simply close their doors and wait. Delays affect passengers, airlines, and many people who rely on air transport. If an emergency is not handled properly, lives could be at risk. That is why every airport has detailed plans and specialized crews to react as soon as they detect a problem.

The Teams That Respond

Several groups at an airport come together to deal with emergencies:

1. **Airport Firefighters**
   These are specialized teams who train for aircraft fires, fuel spills, and other unique hazards. We learned about them in a previous chapter. They have special trucks filled with foam or water and arrive very quickly if a plane has an incident on the runway or a fire starts in a building.
2. **Airport Police or Security Officers**
   These officers handle security threats, suspicious items, and crowd control. If an alarm goes off or if there is an unlawful act, they coordinate with other staff and may involve local police or special units.
3. **Medical and First Aid Staff**
   Some airports have paramedics or medical teams on site. They treat sick or injured travelers and can move them to nearby hospitals if needed.
4. **Operations and Maintenance Crews**
   If there is a sudden runway damage or a power outage, these workers handle repairs, clear debris, and keep the airport functioning.
5. **Air Traffic Control**
   The controllers in the tower or approach radar rooms manage all flights. They guide planes away from trouble spots or direct an emergency flight to land quickly on a cleared runway.
6. **Airlines**
   Each airline has its own employees and resources. If one of their planes needs help, the airline staff work with the airport to make sure the plane is safe and that passengers get assistance.
7. **Local Authorities**
   Some emergencies go beyond the airport's fence. In big incidents, city police, fire departments, or government agencies might also step in. They manage large-scale evacuations, investigate accidents, or set up shelters if needed.

These different teams all follow a master emergency plan. They practice together so they can cooperate smoothly in a real crisis.

The Airport Emergency Plan

Every airport is required to have an emergency plan that covers a wide range of situations. The plan is written in a detailed manual, usually shared with key airport staff, airlines, and local emergency services. It includes:

- **Command Structure**: Who is in charge, and who reports to whom. Typically, there is an Airport Operations Control Center (AOCC) or an incident command post.
- **Communication Rules**: Which radio channels to use, who calls whom, and how to pass information quickly.
- **Response Steps**: Detailed instructions for different emergencies, such as "aircraft crash," "bomb threat," "fuel spill," or "medical outbreak."
- **Evacuation Procedures**: Plans for moving passengers and staff out of buildings or away from runways if a hazard is present.
- **Resource Lists**: Phone numbers for nearby fire stations, hospitals, and utility companies, plus an inventory of equipment like rescue vehicles or portable generators.
- **Training and Drills**: A schedule for practice sessions, so that each group stays familiar with their roles.

This plan helps ensure that no one wastes time deciding what to do when a crisis hits. Everyone already knows their task, from the top manager to the firefighter or police officer on the ground.

Airplane Incidents on the Ground

One of the more common emergencies is a problem with an airplane on the runway or taxiway. For example, a plane might have a tire burst, skid off the pavement in bad weather, or discover smoke in the cabin while still on the ground. In these cases, the airport quickly closes the affected runway or taxiway, and the tower directs other flights away from that area.

Firefighters rush to the scene in their specialized trucks. If there is a fire, they spray foam to contain it. If passengers need to leave the plane, the crew might deploy emergency slides. Medics check for injuries, and the airport's operations team brings buses to move passengers back to the terminal. Meanwhile, airline mechanics or ground support staff might bring equipment to tow the damaged plane away once it is safe.

If the incident is small—like a flat tire—a runway inspection might happen quickly, and the plane can be removed without major disruption. But if the plane is stuck, it can lead to delays. Maintenance crews may need special gear to lift the aircraft. The airport might redirect flights to another runway or even to a different airport if all runways are blocked.

In-Flight Emergencies Leading to Landings

Sometimes, an airplane in the air declares an emergency (called a "Mayday" or "Pan-Pan" call to air traffic control). Reasons can include engine trouble, a medical situation on board, or smoke in the cabin. The pilot requests priority to land as soon as possible. The control tower then puts the airport on alert:

1. **Fire and Rescue Alert**
   Airport firefighters get into position near the runway, ready to respond. If the plane lands safely without further trouble, they simply follow it until it stops. If the landing is rough or there is a fire, the firefighters act immediately.
2. **Clearing the Airspace**
   Air traffic controllers guide other planes away from the runway approach path, giving the troubled plane a direct route to land.
3. **Medical Teams at the Gate**
   If the emergency involves a passenger needing urgent care, an ambulance might wait on the tarmac or at the gate. Sometimes paramedics board the plane right after it stops.
4. **Evacuation if Needed**
   If smoke fills the cabin, the pilot might order an emergency evacuation on the runway. Airport staff help direct people away from the plane to a safe area.
5. **Inspection and Cleanup**
   Once the plane is secured, ground crews check the runway for debris, spilled fuel, or damage to the asphalt. They clean up quickly to reopen the runway.

This coordinated effort can save lives. Pilots know that the airport is prepared and that rescue teams are in place, giving them confidence to bring the plane in fast without risking collisions or delays.

Dealing with Fires in Terminals or Hangars

Fires can break out in terminal buildings, restaurants, shops, or aircraft hangars. Perhaps an electrical fault sparks a small flame behind a shop wall, or an unattended stove in an airport kitchen starts a grease fire. Whatever the cause, the airport firefighting team moves quickly.

Modern airports have many safety features:

- **Smoke Detectors and Sprinklers**
  These detect heat or smoke early and activate alarms. Sprinklers can contain or even extinguish small fires before firefighters arrive.
- **Fire Doors**
  Terminals include heavy doors that automatically close to seal off one area from another, slowing the spread of smoke or flames.
- **Evacuation Routes**
  Signs lead people to exits. Escalators might shut down so people can use stairs. Loud alarms and announcements guide travelers to safe zones or outdoors. Staff help people with disabilities or those unsure of where to go.
- **Backup Generators**
  If a fire knocks out power, the airport's emergency generators keep critical systems (like lights and communications) running.

Because big terminals can hold thousands of people, a quick and organized evacuation is vital. Firefighters then search for anyone left behind, control the flames, and clear away smoke. If the fire is large, local city fire departments may also come. The priority is always to protect lives first.

Medical Emergencies and Public Health

When so many travelers gather, medical issues are bound to happen—heart attacks, fainting spells, allergic reactions, or even widespread illnesses:

1. **First Aid Stations**
   Many airports have medical clinics or first aid desks. If someone feels sick, they can get help without leaving the terminal. Paramedics can handle minor injuries or decide if the person needs hospital care.
2. **Defibrillators (AEDs)**
   Automatic External Defibrillators are placed throughout terminals. If someone's heart stops, staff or bystanders trained in CPR can use an AED to try to restart it. Quick action can save lives.
3. **Contagious Diseases**
   In cases where a traveler might have a serious illness like a highly infectious virus, airport health officers can quarantine that person or direct them to isolation. Airports learned many lessons from global

outbreaks, so they often have scanning or screening for certain diseases. For example, during health scares, some airports check passenger temperatures or ask about travel history.

4. **Ambulance Access**
   Arrangements allow ambulances to reach gates or planes quickly. Some airports have special vehicles or direct routes on the tarmac to bring medical staff right to the aircraft door.

Effective medical support is part of daily airport life, ensuring travelers are not stranded if they fall ill far from home.

Bomb Threats or Security Alerts

Airports pay close attention to security. If someone calls in a bomb threat or a suspicious item is found:

1. **Immediate Assessment**
   Security officers and airport police investigate. They might scan the item, bring bomb-sniffing dogs, or move people away from the area. If it is near a check-in counter, for example, they might block that zone.
2. **Evacuation Decisions**
   If they suspect a real threat, the airport might evacuate terminals or close the runway area. This is a big step because it halts many flights and causes huge delays. But safety comes first.
3. **Special Units**
   Some airports or city police forces have bomb squads trained to defuse or safely detonate suspicious packages. They use protective suits and robots that examine or remove the item.
4. **Communication with Travelers**
   Staff must stay calm, direct people away from danger, and provide clear instructions. Panicked crowds can cause injury, so measured announcements and signage are crucial.
5. **All-Clear or Reopening**
   If experts find no actual bomb or if the item is made safe, the airport reopens. They might do a thorough sweep first, ensuring no other threats remain. Flights then resume, although schedules may be disrupted.

Effective training and well-practiced plans help prevent chaos and ensure people know exactly how to respond.

Natural Disasters and Extreme Weather

Airports are not immune to forces of nature. Tornadoes, earthquakes, floods, hurricanes, or volcanic ash can disrupt flights:

- **Flooding**
  Heavy rain can flood runways or terminals. The airport's drainage system must be strong. Crews might bring pumps or sandbags to protect critical areas. In severe floods, flights may divert to safer airports.
- **Snowstorms and Blizzards**
  Snow can shut runways, cause de-icing delays, or make roads impassable. Snow removal teams work in shifts to keep the runway clear and safe. If the snowfall is too heavy, the airport may have to close temporarily.
- **Hurricanes or Typhoons**
  Strong winds and rain can damage buildings, blow debris onto runways, and risk plane damage. Airports may evacuate, tie down smaller aircraft, or store important vehicles indoors. They also expect power outages, so backup generators become key.
- **Volcanic Ash**
  If a volcano erupts and ash drifts overhead, flights stop. Ash can harm engines. Air traffic control reroutes planes. The airport might keep ground staff on standby until the air is safe for planes again.
- **Earthquakes**
  If the airport is in an earthquake-prone area, buildings and runways might crack. An earthquake can disrupt power, break gas lines, and cause panic. Staff must do rapid inspections before flights can resume.

In such disasters, the airport might also become a hub for emergency relief flights, bringing in supplies or rescue workers.

Hazardous Materials Incidents

Airports handle hazardous goods—chemicals, flammable liquids, batteries, medical isotopes, and more. If a container leaks:

1. **Containment**
   Staff isolate the spill area, wearing protective gear if the material is toxic or corrosive. They use barriers or absorbents to keep it from spreading into drains or the soil.

2. **Notification**
   Police, firefighters, or hazmat teams arrive. If a large-scale danger is possible, the airport warns nearby communities or environmental agencies.
3. **Cleanup**
   Trained specialists remove the spilled substance, wash the area with neutralizers if needed, and dispose of waste safely. If runways or taxiways are affected, flights might be delayed until it is safe.
4. **Investigations**
   Once stable, officials check how the spill happened. Maybe the packaging was faulty, or staff mislabeled the goods. Lessons learned help prevent repeats.

Because many cargo shipments contain items like battery packs or chemicals, proper labeling and secure packing are critical. Airport authorities enforce strict rules to lower the risk of a hazardous spill.

Cybersecurity Emergencies

Modern airports rely on computers for flight schedules, security systems, baggage sorting, and communications. If hackers attack or a critical system fails:

- **System Shutdowns**
  Airport screens might go blank, or security checkpoints might not function. This can create confusion, leading to flight delays and possibly security gaps.
- **Backup Plans**
  Airports store essential data offline or have duplicate systems to keep operations going. For example, if the main baggage system is hacked, staff might switch to a manual or smaller backup system.
- **IT Teams**
  Specialized information technology staff jump into action to trace the breach, block it, and restore normal service. They might work with government cyber agencies if the attack is severe.
- **Protecting Passenger Data**
  Airports store personal details from flight bookings or Wi-Fi users. A breach could expose that info, so firewalls, encryption, and staff training help reduce these risks.

Cyberattacks can be less visible than a plane crash or fire, but they can shut down an airport just as effectively if not managed well.

Emergency Drills and Practice

Large airports hold regular drills—some small, some large—to practice. For instance:

- **Tabletop Exercises**
  Key managers and emergency chiefs gather around a table. They walk through a scenario, like "Plane X has landed short of the runway." They discuss step by step who does what. This checks if the plan is current and if any confusion arises in the chain of command.
- **Full-Scale Exercises**
  These happen every year or two, involving actual fire trucks, ambulances, volunteers acting as injured passengers, and so on. The scenario might be a simulated aircraft crash on the runway. Observers note if staff follow procedures correctly or if communication fails.
- **Partial Drills**
  Sometimes the airport only tests a specific area—like an evacuation of part of the terminal, or a medical scenario in a gate lounge. Smaller drills can happen more often and let staff practice particular skills.

After each drill, they do a debriefing. What went right? What was slow or confusing? This feedback updates the emergency plan, so the airport is always improving its readiness.

Communicating with the Public During Crisis

When things go wrong, everyone wants to know what is happening. Airports manage many channels:

1. **Announcements**
   Loudspeakers inform travelers of any changes, telling them whether flights are delayed, gates are changed, or if they must evacuate. Staff speak calmly and clearly.
2. **Information Desks and Screens**
   Terminal screens might show messages like "Emergency in progress,

please follow directions." Staff at information desks also receive updates to answer questions.

3. **Social Media**
   The airport's official accounts on social media can give real-time notices: "Runway closed due to incident," or "Departures delayed." This helps families or travelers at home see the situation.

4. **Media Briefings**
   In a serious event, the airport's spokesperson or director might hold a press conference, giving basic facts about what happened, how many flights are affected, and if there are injuries. They avoid sharing speculation or unverified details.

Keeping the public informed reduces panic, stops rumors, and ensures people know what steps to take. Even in tense moments, clear communication is a powerful tool.

Handling Stranded Travelers

Some emergencies force flight cancellations or closures. Hundreds or thousands of passengers might be stuck for hours or days:

- **Providing Essentials**
  Airports and airlines might hand out blankets, bottled water, and simple snacks. If the terminal restrooms become crowded, staff keep them clean and restocked.
- **Overnight Shelters**
  If flights are canceled overnight, travelers might sleep on benches or cots. Larger airports have cots in storage for such situations. Local hotels might fill up quickly, so some people have no choice but to stay at the airport.
- **Rebooking**
  Airline staff rebook passengers on later flights or direct them to other airports if possible. Good communication helps people understand their options and keep calm.
- **Helping Vulnerable Passengers**
  Elderly travelers, families with babies, or people needing special assistance might need more care. Staff ensure they have a comfortable place to rest, access to medical help, and priority rebooking if possible.

It is not a pleasant experience, but thorough emergency planning can ease the disruption until normal service returns.

Investigations After Major Incidents

If a big emergency happens, like a crash or serious security event, official investigations follow:

- **Accident Investigation**
  Experts from aviation authorities and aircraft manufacturers inspect the wreckage or flight data to find what went wrong. This can take months. The airport cooperates by providing records, radar info, or ground staff statements.
- **Security Analysis**
  If it was a security breach, officials check how it happened. Did someone skip a checkpoint? Was screening equipment faulty? They then change rules or retrain staff to avoid a repeat.
- **Incident Reports**
  The airport writes a detailed report on how the emergency was managed. It logs how quickly teams arrived, whether communications worked, how resources were used, and so on.
- **Lessons Learned**
  These findings often lead to improvements in equipment, training, or procedures. For instance, if an emergency response took too long to reach a certain spot, the airport might build a new road or station vehicles closer.

Investigations are not about blame alone; they focus on preventing future issues. Airports and airlines share these lessons widely.

Crisis Centers and Leadership

In a big event, the airport might activate a Crisis Management Center. This is a secure room with screens, phones, and computers showing live data—like flight tracks, CCTV views, or weather. The crisis leader (often an airport executive) gathers all department heads:

- **Fire Chief**
  Reports on rescue efforts, what is under control, what help they need.

- **Security Chief**
  Updates on crowd control, any suspicious activity, or if more police are needed.
- **Operations Manager**
  Checks if runways are open, gates are free, and how many flights must be diverted.
- **Airline Reps**
  Share info on planes in the air, passenger rosters, or planned schedules.
- **Communications Officer**
  Handles announcements, social media, and media requests.

This central hub keeps everyone in sync. They decide if the airport stays partially open or fully closes, how to handle incoming flights, or if they need help from external agencies. Once the crisis subsides, they scale back the center's operations.

Protecting Airport Technology and Power

An airport's power supply is crucial—everything from runway lights to baggage belts depends on electricity. In an emergency:

1. **Backup Generators**
   Many airports have strong backup systems that turn on if the main power grid fails. These can run key areas like control towers, terminals, or cargo handling.
2. **Uninterruptible Power Supplies (UPS)**
   Critical systems like computer servers or radar screens have UPS batteries. Even a brief blackout could cause data loss or confusion, so these batteries keep them running until generators start.
3. **Fuel Reserves**
   Generators need fuel, so the airport stores enough to last hours or days.
4. **Protecting IT Networks**
   If a fire or flood threatens the server rooms, staff might move servers to a safe location or switch to a remote backup. Good planning ensures flight data or security systems do not vanish in a crisis.

Securing power and technology means planes can continue to land safely, communications remain online, and travelers get the information they need.

Helping the Surrounding Community

In some emergencies, the airport itself is fine, but the local area might be in trouble. Examples:

- **Major Earthquake or Hurricane**
  Roads, hospitals, or power lines around the city may be damaged. The airport can become a staging area for relief flights bringing food, water, or rescue teams. It might also accept helicopters carrying supplies to remote zones.
- **Chemical or Industrial Accident**
  If there is a toxic spill near the airport, the airport might open extra facilities to shelter evacuees from the community. Or it might close runways if there is a risk of fumes affecting planes.
- **Host to Evacuation Flights**
  If a region is in crisis, some people may need to leave quickly. The airport helps coordinate special flights to move them to safer places.

Airports are large, well-connected sites with strong infrastructure. In times of local or regional disasters, they often serve as lifelines.

Terror Threats or Unlawful Acts

In very serious crises, such as a hijacking or sabotage attempt, the airport's plans expand:

1. **Lockdowns**
   Specific terminals, gates, or runways may be locked down to keep people safe. Police or special response teams take charge.
2. **Negotiations**
   If a plane is taken over, specialized negotiators might talk with the hijackers. The airport sets aside a secure zone for them to work. Meanwhile, the rest of the airport may partially function unless the threat is widespread.
3. **Passenger and Crew Safety**
   The airline, security, and rescue teams plan how to protect or free hostages. This might involve discreet operations. Only if absolutely necessary do they move toward a forced rescue, and that is typically run by national security forces.

4. **Airport-Wide Security Measures**
   Sometimes all flights are suspended while authorities check planes, passenger lists, or baggage for further threats.

Although rare, these scenarios require advanced preparedness and close cooperation between the airport and national security forces.

Putting It All Together

Emergency handling at an airport is a huge responsibility. From minor issues like a small leak of hazardous cargo to big events like an airplane crash, staff must stay calm, follow the emergency plan, and communicate clearly. Rescue teams, security officers, air traffic control, and many others join forces to protect lives and limit damage.

The airport emergency plan is at the heart of this readiness. Detailed instructions, training drills, and continuous updates keep everyone aware of what to do. Firefighters and police practice for fires, suspicious packages, or medical crises. Air traffic controllers plan flight routes for incoming emergencies and coordinate safe skies. Terminal staff learn to guide passengers if they must evacuate, and maintenance teams fix damage to runways or buildings so normal operations can resume.

CHAPTER 20: THE NEXT STEPS FOR AIRPORTS

Airports have changed a lot over the years. They began as small airfields with simple terminals. Today, they are giant hubs that handle millions of travelers, complex cargo operations, and advanced security systems. As technology progresses and the world keeps changing, airports face new demands. In this final chapter, we will explore how airports might evolve. We will discuss future technologies and designs, how airports might become more comfortable and efficient, and the ways they can continue to serve communities around the globe.

Smart Airports: Using Technology

Many airports already use some level of automation, but this could expand drastically in the coming years:

1. **Biometric Boarding**
   You might not need a paper boarding pass in the future. Instead, cameras scan your face, matching it with your passport photo and ticket in a secure database. This can speed up check-in and boarding.

2. **Self-Service Everywhere**
   Self-check-in kiosks, self-bag drops, and automated passport gates could become more common. That means fewer lines and less waiting.
3. **Robots and AI**
   Robots might clean floors, deliver food, or guide lost travelers. Artificial intelligence could monitor cameras to spot suspicious activity or track crowd flows, adjusting lines in real time.
4. **Augmented Reality (AR) Apps**
   Imagine wearing smart glasses or using a phone app that overlays directions or flight details onto the real-world view of the terminal. You could follow arrows right on your screen to find your gate or baggage carousel.
5. **Predictive Maintenance**
   Advanced sensors on escalators, jet bridges, or runway lighting might warn staff before a part fails. This reduces unexpected breakdowns and flight delays.

While high-tech airports sound efficient, concerns about data privacy and job changes remain. We may see balanced approaches that keep staff involved for human help and warmth while technology handles routine tasks.

Passenger Experience: Comfort and Ease

Air travel can be stressful, but airports aim to make it smoother:

- **Streamlined Security**
  Future scanners could allow you to keep electronics and liquids in your bag. Body scanners might become faster and less intrusive. This cuts down on lines.
- **Seamless Connections**
  If flights connect, your bag might move automatically to the next plane, and you could pass from one gate to another with minimal hassle. Some airports already have programs that automatically transfer your luggage without re-checking it.
- **Health and Well-Being**
  Airports might expand quiet lounges, nap pods, spa services, or even small fitness areas. Travelers waiting for a long layover could rest, exercise, or take part in wellness activities rather than just sitting in a chair.

- **Family-Friendly Zones**
  More dedicated play areas for children, private nursing rooms for new mothers, or family seating sections might appear. This helps parents keep kids happy and calm during travel.
- **Digital Personal Assistants**
  A phone app might track your flight, gate changes, or delays in real time, offering suggestions like, "Grab a snack at X store on your way," or "It's a 12-minute walk to your gate—head there now." This eliminates confusion about gate changes.

These features focus on making the terminal a pleasant space rather than just a place to wait in line.

Reducing Environmental Impact

We discussed green efforts in Chapter 18. This area will only grow more important:

1. **Net-Zero or Carbon-Neutral Goals**
   Many airports aim to produce net-zero emissions for ground operations by a certain date (for example, 2030 or 2050). They will invest in solar panels, wind energy, and energy-saving designs.
2. **Electric or Hybrid Planes**
   Short-haul electric planes might appear in the next two decades. Airports could build charging stations for them, just like electric car chargers, but on a larger scale.
3. **Green Building Materials**
   Future terminals might be made with low-carbon concrete, recycled steel, or sustainable wood. Big open spaces could rely on natural ventilation and daylight to cut energy costs.
4. **Sustainable Fuels and Airlines**
   More airports will offer sustainable aviation fuel. Some might require airlines to use a small percentage of SAF in each flight. This helps reduce the carbon footprint of flying.

By prioritizing these steps, airports can align with global efforts to slow climate change. Over time, they might transform from heavy energy users into eco-friendly transport hubs.

Multi-Modal Travel Hubs

In the future, airports might not be just for airplanes. They could become broader "mobility centers":

- **High-Speed Trains**
  Large airports in Europe and Asia already have train stations. Future expansions could link airports to bullet trains, allowing travelers to move quickly between cities without needing a car or short flights.
- **Hyperloops**
  This technology is still being tested, but it imagines pods traveling through low-pressure tubes at very high speeds. If it becomes real, airports could connect to major city centers or other airports by hyperloop routes.
- **Air Taxis**
  Electric vertical takeoff and landing (eVTOL) craft might shuttle passengers from downtown rooftops to the airport. That reduces road congestion. A special "vertiport" area in the airport could handle these craft.
- **Shared Mobility Services**
  Car-sharing, ride-hailing, and on-demand buses might have integrated booking through the airport's website. One ticket might cover your flight and the ride from your home to the airport, making travel more seamless.

The goal is to let travelers pick the best mode of transport for each leg of their trip, merging trains, eVTOLs, or buses with airline flights for an easier experience.

Urban Airports and Mega-Airports

Different airports may follow different paths:

1. **Urban Landing Spots**
   City-based airports with short runways might specialize in smaller planes, business jets, or eVTOL traffic. They focus on quick connections for travelers who want to be near downtown.
2. **Giant Hubs**
   Huge airports in major cities serve as global connectors. With multiple runways and terminals, they may keep growing. They might add more

"satellite" concourses connected by trains or underground tunnels. Some airports already have terminals that look like small cities, with hotels, malls, and offices.

3. **Parallel Runway Systems**
   To handle more flights, large airports might build pairs of parallel runways, letting them land and take off simultaneously. Advanced air traffic control reduces spacing so planes can move more efficiently.
4. **Decentralized Check-In**
   Some experts suggest that check-in and baggage drop might move to city centers or train stations. People could drop their suitcases before even arriving at the airport. Then they board a fast train or shuttle that takes them directly to their plane's gate.
5. **Remote Towers**
   Smaller airports may not need a traditional control tower on site. Controllers could operate from a central facility far away, watching live video feeds and radar. This can save cost and help staff handle multiple small airports at once.

Virtual and Remote Experiences

Strangely enough, some travelers may skip airports entirely if virtual reality or advanced communication tools keep improving. Business meetings might happen in realistic VR rooms, reducing the need for short-haul flights. Still, people will keep traveling for fun, family visits, or seeing places in person. But the rise of better internet and VR might reduce some business flight demand.

For airports themselves:

- **Training**
  Staff might use VR for emergency drills or to learn how to operate complex equipment without risking real planes.
- **Passenger Tours**
  If a traveler is anxious about flying, a VR experience could show them the plane's interior, safety demos, and what to expect at security checkpoints. This could ease stress.
- **Design Preview**
  Before building a new terminal, architects create a virtual model. Airport managers and the public might "walk" through it digitally, giving feedback on layout and signage. This reduces costly mistakes in real construction.

Though not all experiences can go virtual, these tools help airports plan and educate travelers in a more interactive way.

Data Sharing and Collaboration

Airports rely on information from many sources—airlines, weather stations, cargo handlers, security teams. Soon, advanced data systems might merge all these streams:

- **Real-Time Flight Updates**
  Everyone, from the airline gate agent to the taxi driver waiting outside, could see exactly when a plane will land, the passenger load, or if a bag is delayed. This reduces guesswork and confusion.
- **Predictive Operations**
  By analyzing patterns, an airport might forecast busy times at security or immigration, then open more lanes or direct staff accordingly. If storms are approaching, the system might proactively reschedule flights to prevent a chaotic last-minute scramble.
- **Blockchain for Cargo**
  Cargo shipments might use blockchain technology to track items from origin to plane to destination. This ensures security and transparency for shipments like medical supplies or electronics.
- **Health Data**
  In times of disease concerns, airports might share screening data or temperature checks with health agencies, tracking the spread of illness while respecting privacy rules.

As data flows more freely, operations can become smoother. The main challenge is balancing privacy, security, and the convenience of open information.

Safety and Security: Evolving Threats

Security checks have grown more complex over time. New concerns might emerge:

1. **Non-Metal Threats**
   Future scanners must detect not just metal weapons, but also explosives in liquids or 3D-printed items that might not show on old machines.

2. **Behavior Recognition**
   AI systems might spot unusual body language or facial expressions in real time. Some airports already use "behavior detection officers" trained to watch for signs of stress or wrongdoing. AI could help, but raises privacy questions.
3. **Cybersecurity**
   More digital systems mean hackers could attempt to disrupt flights or sabotage data. Constant vigilance with firewalls, encryption, and backups will be needed.
4. **Drones**
   Small drones near airports can interfere with flights. Future solutions may include drone detection radars or geofencing that blocks them from flying in approach paths. Some airports might have "drone defense" systems that intercept or disable unauthorized drones.
5. **Biosecurity**
   As global travel increases, the spread of new viruses can happen quickly. Airports might keep disease screening methods ready. Quarantine areas, rapid tests, and contact tracing tools could become routine if an outbreak occurs.

Staying ahead of these threats requires ongoing staff training and updates to equipment. This ensures airports remain safe places where travelers can move without fear.

Luggage and Baggage Innovations

Baggage handling has come a long way, but more improvements are possible:

- **Automatic Tagging**
  You might attach a small digital chip to your bag once and use it for multiple trips. It updates flight details through an app. The bag can track itself and tell you where it is.
- **Robot Delivery**
  Robots or conveyor belts that run under floors might bring checked bags directly to the plane. Or a small robot could deliver your suitcase to a baggage carousel for pick-up.
- **Smart Lockers**
  If you have a layover, you could store your carry-on in a secure locker

that locks electronically. With your phone or fingerprint, you retrieve it when ready.
- **Less Need for Checked Bags**
Some travelers might have essential items shipped by cargo ahead of time, or they may rent clothes or gear at their destination. This can reduce baggage lines at the airport. But this depends on how convenient or cost-effective shipping is.

Overall, the aim is to cut mishandled luggage and speed up the time from check-in to departure.

Focus on Wellness and Layout

Tomorrow's airport designs could emphasize calmness and well-being:

- **Spacious Interiors**
Instead of cramped waiting areas, designs might use open layouts with comfortable seating, natural light, and greeneries to reduce stress.
- **Quiet Zones**
Special spaces with dim lighting and soundproofing for people who need silence—very useful for travelers with sensory sensitivities.
- **Cultural Displays**
Airports can highlight local art or history. Passengers might explore small exhibits, making the wait more enjoyable. This also helps them learn about the region.
- **Healthy Food and Local Eateries**
Future terminals might push out junk food stands in favor of healthier meal options or local specialties. Organic, farm-to-table or low-waste restaurants could become the norm, reflecting public demand for better food choices.
- **Outdoor Terraces**
Some modern airports feature open-air decks where travelers can get fresh air or enjoy plane spotting. If security rules permit, these spaces can reduce the feeling of being stuck inside.

By mixing comfort with functional design, airports can become places passengers do not dread, but rather find interesting or even relaxing to explore.

Personalized Services

Using data about your flight, preferences, or frequent flyer status, airports could tailor services:

- **Adaptive Signs**
  Digital signboards might shift language based on the majority of nearby passengers' native languages, or personal devices might trigger them to show your gate info if you step close.
- **Upgrades and Offers**
  If your flight is delayed, an airport app might send a voucher for a free coffee at a nearby cafe. Or if you have time, it might suggest a spa discount to help you pass the waiting period.
- **Assisted Navigation**
  A traveler in a wheelchair might get an alert that a staff member is ready to guide them, or a family with children might see a route leading past a play area. This level of personalization ensures each group's unique needs are met.
- **Language and Translation**
  In terminals with advanced AI, real-time translation tools can display or speak flight announcements in multiple tongues. This helps travelers who are not fluent in the local language.

Balancing personalization with privacy will be crucial. Some people may prefer anonymity over customized perks.

Economic and Social Impacts

As airports grow, they can shape the economy around them:

- **Job Creation**
  Big airports employ tens of thousands. Future expansions or new technologies might change job types (for example, more IT experts, fewer manual check-in clerks).
- **Community Collaboration**
  Airports might partner with local schools or colleges, offering internships in aviation or hospitality. This fosters local talent and goodwill.
- **Reduced Noise**
  As planes become quieter, expansions might be more acceptable to

neighbors. Still, open dialogue about flight paths, times, and insulation is vital to keep good relations with the nearby community.

- **Support for Tourism**
  A state-of-the-art airport can attract travelers, boosting local hotels, restaurants, and events. The airport often becomes a region's "front door," so an appealing design and efficient services can improve the area's reputation.

Future airports could be major hubs for economic activity, but they also must respect residents' quality of life and the environment.

Collaborations Between Airports

Airports do not exist in isolation. They might form networks to share:

- **Best Practices**
  If one airport finds a better method of scanning baggage or a greener way to run air conditioning, it can help others. This collective learning speeds up industry progress.
- **Flight Coordination**
  Busy regions have multiple airports that coordinate schedules to avoid airspace congestion. They might also share data about weather or runway conditions so planes can divert smoothly if needed.
- **Regional Planning**
  If a new airport is being built, existing airports might shift flights around. Cargo traffic might move to one site, while passenger flights go to another. This can reduce duplication of large expansions if the region plans together.
- **Emergency Assistance**
  In a major crisis, one airport might lend firefighting equipment or staff to another. International cooperation among airports is sometimes arranged through memoranda or industry groups.

These links help airports adapt quickly and manage big changes that go beyond a single terminal's walls.

Faster Connections, Fewer Lines

Long lines for check-in, security, or immigration can be reduced by:

1. **Off-Airport Check-In**
   Checking bags in at hotels or city kiosks, so by the time you arrive at the airport, you go straight to security.
2. **E-Gates**
   Facial recognition gates for immigration can speed up border checks, especially if travelers are pre-registered.
3. **Sensor-Driven Security**
   Instead of stopping each person, advanced scanners might discreetly scan the whole crowd, flagging only specific individuals for extra checks if suspicious items are detected.
4. **Real-Time Wait Estimates**
   Apps or large screens show you the current waiting time at each security checkpoint. You pick the shortest one. This spreads passenger flow evenly.

As these technologies improve, the typical "hurry up and wait" at airports might fade, replaced by more efficient processes.

Handling Future Pandemics or Health Crises

The recent global events taught airports new lessons about disease prevention:

- **Health Screenings**
  Temperature checks or quick tests might become standard in times of high alert. Some airports might have permanent thermal cameras to identify passengers with fever.
- **Touchless Systems**
  Automated doors, check-in machines with face recognition, and voice-activated kiosks reduce the need to touch shared surfaces.
- **Enhanced Cleaning**
  Robots could disinfect seats, railings, or bathrooms with UV light or spray solutions. Frequent cleaning of high-touch zones continues.
- **Isolation Areas**
  A dedicated zone to hold passengers from high-risk flights, letting medical staff screen them before they enter the main terminal. This might stop viruses from spreading to everyone else.

Airports remain key points for detecting and controlling global outbreaks. Advanced health measures could become normal practice, even after crises end.

The Human Touch: Customer Service

Amid all the automation, human helpers will still matter:

- **Trained Staff**
Friendly, knowledgeable employees remain a big plus. Whether it is a lost traveler needing directions or someone with a special need, a real person's empathy and kindness are irreplaceable.
- **Personal Guides**
Some airports offer "meet and greet" services. In the future, these might expand. If you pay a bit extra, a personal assistant meets you at the curb, whisks you through check-in, and escorts you to a lounge or gate. This service might be more common or even become a standard part of premium tickets.
- **Ambassadors for Tech**
With so many new gadgets, staff might help older passengers or less tech-savvy travelers use e-gates, digital baggage tags, or phone apps. This ensures no one is left behind by the digital shift.
- **Conflict Resolution**
When flights are canceled or disruptions happen, staff who can calmly solve problems on the spot are essential. People appreciate empathetic employees who go the extra mile.

No matter how advanced airports get, the caring presence of real staff will keep travelers comfortable, especially in stressful moments.

Cargo Innovations

Air cargo will keep evolving as e-commerce grows:

- **Automated Warehouses**
Robot arms and conveyor systems can sort packages rapidly, scanning barcodes or RFID tags. This speeds up shipping and lowers errors.
- **Drones for Last-Mile Delivery**
After a cargo plane lands, swarms of small drones might deliver items directly to local addresses. This system is still in testing, but it may become normal in certain areas.
- **Digital Customs**
Paperwork for imports and exports might go fully digital. Customs

officers use AI to screen shipments for illegal or unsafe items quickly. The entire cargo process becomes faster and more secure.
- **Cool Chain**
For perishables like food or vaccines, improved containers maintain precise temperatures. Smart sensors inside each box alert staff if temperature limits are exceeded.

Airports with high-tech cargo facilities will be competitive, attracting global trade and making shipping more reliable for businesses.

Investing in Runway and Airspace Capacity

Even the best terminal technology will not help if the runway is overloaded. Future changes:

- **More Runways**
Some busy airports might add runways to handle increased flights. But land availability and noise concerns can block such expansions.
- **Upgraded Air Traffic Control**
Satellite-based systems like ADS-B (Automatic Dependent Surveillance-Broadcast) let controllers space planes more efficiently. Planes might follow precise routes that allow more aircraft in the same airspace safely.
- **Mixed-Mode Operations**
With advanced technology, an airport might use one runway for both landings and takeoffs simultaneously, as long as safety is maintained. This can raise the maximum flight capacity without building a new runway.
- **Regional or Secondary Airports**
If major airports cannot expand, some traffic shifts to smaller regional ones. Low-cost carriers or cargo might move there, freeing capacity at the main hub.

These steps keep delays low as air travel demand grows, though each option has cost and environmental concerns.

Faster Security and Border Crossings

As countries tighten border controls for safety, airports look for ways to keep lines short:

1. **Preclearance**
   Some travelers might complete immigration checks before boarding, especially if there is a special deal between countries. On arrival, they skip the usual passport line.
2. **E-Passports**
   Modern passports have chips storing biometric data. Border checkpoints can read these quickly, matching your face to the passport photo. The entire process might take seconds.
3. **Risk-Based Screening**
   Trusted traveler programs let low-risk passengers pass simpler checks, while security focuses on unknown or higher-risk individuals. This approach can reduce overall congestion.
4. **Face or Fingerprint Recognition**
   Instead of stamps, your fingerprint or face image could be logged digitally. If you revisit the same country, the border system recognizes you instantly, assuming all is in order.

Though these systems can raise privacy debates, they also speed up international travel and improve security checks.

Bringing It All Together

Airports will keep changing to serve people better. From faster check-ins and more comfortable waiting areas to greener designs and improved emergency plans, the next decades promise plenty of updates. Some airports may lead the way with cutting-edge solutions—biometric gates, electric planes, or advanced cargo robotics. Others might stick to simpler upgrades, focusing on better passenger flow and expansions. But all share the goal of balancing safety, convenience, and community welfare.

Key points for the future:

- **Technology**: Smarter scanning, self-service, data analytics, and possibly AI in everyday airport operations.
- **Sustainability**: More solar panels, electric ground fleets, recycling, and possibly electric or hybrid aircraft for short routes.
- **Passenger Comfort**: Less waiting, better seating, meaningful experiences like quiet zones or family play areas.

- **Community and Environment**: Managing noise, emissions, and local development responsibly.
- **Adaptability**: Being ready for new threats, public health crises, or changes in travel patterns.

The airport has become more than a place to catch flights. It is a meeting ground for travelers worldwide, a hub of technology and logistics, and sometimes even a cultural showcase for the region. While challenges like congestion, security, and environmental impact remain, airports push forward with creative strategies and teamwork. Through innovation and cooperation—among airlines, airport authorities, governments, and travelers themselves—airports continue to evolve as vital gateways that connect our planet.

That concludes our exploration of how airports work and where they may be headed. From runways and control towers to maintenance crews, baggage systems, and futuristic ideas, we have seen how every part fits together to keep people flying safely and efficiently. The next time you walk through an airport, you can appreciate the many steps, systems, and dedicated workers behind each flight. Airports truly are remarkable places—engines of mobility that bring our world closer.

Help Us Share Your Thoughts!

Dear reader,

Thank you for spending your time with this book. We hope it brought you enjoyment and a few new ideas to think about. If there was anything that didn't work for you, or if you have suggestions on how we can improve, please let us know at **kontakt@skriuwer.com**. Your feedback means a lot to us and helps us make our books even better.

If you enjoyed this book, we would be very grateful if you left a review on the site where you purchased it. Your review not only helps other readers find our books, but also encourages us to keep creating more stories and materials that you'll love.

By choosing Skriuwer, you're also supporting **Frisian**—a minority language mainly spoken in the northern Netherlands. Although **Frisian** has a rich history, the number of speakers is shrinking, and it's at risk of dying out. Your purchase helps fund resources to preserve and promote this language, such as educational programs and learning tools. If you'd like to learn more about Frisian or even start learning it yourself, please visit **www.learnfrisian.com**.

Thank you for being part of our community. We look forward to sharing more books with you in the future.

Warm regards,
The Skriuwer Team

www.ingramcontent.com/pod-product-compliance
Lightning Source LLC
Chambersburg PA
CBHW082246220526
45469CB00009B/2893